THE
LITTLE
BOOK
OF
ESSEX

DEE GORDON

First published 2009

The History Press
The Mill, Brimscombe Port
Stroud, Gloucestershire, GL5 2QG
www.thehistorypress.co.uk

Reprinted 2010, 2012, 2015

British Library Cataloguing in Publication Data.
A catalogue record for this book is available from the British Library.

ISBN 978 0 7509 5127 2
Typesetting and origination by The History Press
Printed in Great Britain by TJ International.

CONTENTS

INTRODUCTION

Over a recent ten-year period, the population of Essex has increased at a higher rate than anywhere else in the country. For those of us who live here, this is absolutely understandable. So often unfairly maligned, the county has a fascinating history and is full of fascinating places and fascinating people. It is a county bordering London and reaches the eastern coast, London's nearest beach being that at Leigh-on-Sea. Whether an Essex resident or a visitor, there is a lot more out there than is available in local history books or tourist information centres. Trying to assemble a diverse array of lesser-known insights into a county that so many people think they 'know' (even if they've never been to Essex), has been challenging, time-consuming but utterly worthwhile. The research has provided such diverse snippets as:

In AD 587 the Kingdom of Essex incorporated Hertfordshire and Middlesex, and the capital city of Essex was London. King Aescwine, the first king of the independent Saxon Kingdom of Essex, ruled for sixty years.

The fifty richest Essex people are worth collectively £6 billion according to the 2007 *Essex Life* rich list, with Alan Sugar predictably at the top.

The Maldon Embroidery on display at St Peter's Tower in Maldon's High Street took three years and eighty-three embroideresses to complete. It is 42ft long and shows the history of the town and the surrounding area from the coming of the Vikings.

In 1215, four Essex barons were among those (twenty-five in all) who forced King John to put his name to the Magna Carta, the thirteenth-century founding statement of the rights of man.

There are seventy-two listed red telephone boxes in Essex including a matching pair in Epping and a row of three in Maldon.

It is possible to walk by field paths across Essex from the outskirts of London to the sea at Harwich or Bradwell-on-Sea.

THE SEARCH FOR OLYMPIC TALENT.
A PATRIOTIC FARMER TURNS A FIERCE BULL INTO A FIELD IN ORDER TO TEST THE HURDLING POSSIBILITIES OF HIS FARM-HANDS.

The first ever British Olympic champion was an Essex resident, Launceston Elliot. In 1896 he won a gold medal in Athens for a single-handed lift of 71kg in the weight-lifting final and silver for the two-handed lift. Elliot was also the first British athlete to compete in an Olympics as he took part in the first event, the heats for the 100 metres on 6 April 1896, an event in which he failed to qualify, finishing fourth.

Dunmow Priory in Essex is said to be the resting-place of Robin Hood's Maid Marian but, sadly, all that remains of the priory is the present church of Dunmow.

A survey of 1,000 young people aged 18–30, conducted by Sony BMG in 2008, revealed that Southend-on-Sea is the top place in the UK for fun and holiday romance.

Chocolate boxes and biscuit tins carry fewer pictures of Essex than of any other county.

TOWNS AND VILLAGES, STREETS AND BUILDINGS

AROUND THE COUNTY

There are 14,000 listed buildings in the county compared to 13,000 in Suffolk and 10,000 in Norfolk, both of which have larger geographical areas. Of these, 240 are in Thurrock and over 200 in Coggeshall.

A nineteenth-century Italian-style manor built on the site of Pyrgo Palace, Havering-atte-Bower (pulled down in the eighteenth century) had every conceivable mod-con including its own gasworks.

The villagers of Manewdon (now Manuden), Farnham, Elsenham, Stansted and Ugley fought against the national boundary commission in 1888 who wanted to reclassify the villages as being in Hertfordshire, not Essex. The villagers won their argument and remain proud to be in Essex.

Southend-on-Sea has one of the only planetariums outside London; it is based within the town's central museum.

Palaeolithic stone tools have been found in Essex indicating that humans have lived in the area ever since the first Ice Age. As at the 2001 census, the population of Essex was 1,310,922.

The name Essex originates from East Seaxe or East Saxons, the land of the East Saxons. The county emblem features, a tad alarmingly, three seaxes, a single-edged knife or sword.

Ingatestone and Brentwood have been listed in the *Telegraph*'s top twenty richest towns in Britain, while Chelmsford has been listed as number eight in the top twenty places to live by the television programme *Location, Location, Location* (2007), with Barking and Dagenham at number fourteen of the worst twenty! Castle Point (comprising Canvey Island, Benfleet, Thundersley, Hadleigh) has the highest density of owner-occupiers in the country at 89 per cent, compared to a UK average of 70 per cent.

Finchingfield is reputed to be the most photographed village in England, and has inspired painters such as Lucien Pisarro and Alfred Munnings. Honeypot Cottage in the village has been immortalised in the Lilliput Lane series of porcelain models.

The Naze Tower at Walton on the Naze is believed to be the only one of its kind in the country. It was built in 1721, originally as a marker for ships approaching Harwich harbour, and stands 86ft tall.

Frinton was unique among seaside resorts in not having a pub; not until 2000 that is, when the Lock and Barrel opened despite residential objections. Perhaps more quaintly, even the rustic public toilets on the Greensward have a thatched roof.

St Osyth has the only naturist beach in Essex (although there is a naturist camp at Springwood, near Colchester).

The post office at Good Easter used to have a thriving trade during Holy Week from people who wished to have Good Easter stamped on their Easter cards.

Essex has a coastline that stretches well over 350 miles. The resorts of Dovercourt, Frinton, Walton on the Naze, Clacton-on-Sea, St Osyth and Brightlingsea are known collectively as the Essex Sunshine Coast.

THE UNEXPECTED – AND THE DOWNRIGHT CONFUSING

Hatfield Heath, 4 miles inside the Essex border, has a Hertfordshire postcode.

When the Ragged School Union began organising visits to Epping Forest for parties of poor children from the East End (in 1891), the area became known as Lousy Loughton from the lice and fleas said to be left behind. Local streets and parts of the forest were sprayed with disinfectant after the children passed through, but neither this, nor the undignified mode of travel from London with metal identity tags and being locked into train carriages, stopped the children from having fun.

Ramsey Island, near Bradwell-on-Sea, is not an island. Nor is Foulness Island, alongside Shoeburyness.

Chelmsford, the county town of Essex since 1250, is not a city in spite of it having a cathedral, and a football team called Chelmsford City. In recent years, it became the first town (or city) in Essex to be declared a Fairtrade town, dedicated to achieving a fairer deal for farmers and producers in the developing world.

When one of the largest oak trees in Britain, known as the Fairlop Oak, died in 1820 (in Hainault Forest), part of its timber was used to make a pulpit and a reading desk for London's St Pancras Church, Euston Road.

Basildon Hall is reputedly the only stately home to ever be blown up by a bottle of whisky. In 1834, after the former palace had downgraded to service as an inn, a travelling salesman fell into a drunken sleep alongside a lighted candle and an uncorked bottle of whisky. The whisky fumes ignited, causing an explosion and fire that destroyed the building and killed the salesman and a woman in the next room. The building, which stood on Clicketts Hill, has since been demolished.

Wanstead Meeting House (for Quakers) was formerly an archery pavilion and an assembly room where Dickens gave a reading and where William Morris's sister met her former husband.

The Temple in the middle of Wanstead Park is the only building still standing that was associated with Wanstead House – but it was not a temple. It was a place for banqueting and entertainment, dating from before 1830.

A bungalow in Lower Dunton Road, Laindon, was the drop-off and collection point until the 1950s for the muddy wellingtons of those commuters living in the Basildon 'plotlands' (pre the New Town) en route to Laindon station. When the property changed hands, the new owners were more than a little perplexed by the filthy footwear appearing on their doorstep.

The expression 'Where's Wally?' seems to have started out as a genuine announcement on the public address system at the Weeley Rock Festival near Clacton, in August 1971, when Wally had been separated from his friends.

The 'secret' nuclear bunker at Kelvedon Hatch, a relic of the Cold War, is no longer a secret. It was hidden behind an innocuous 1950s bungalow, via a 350ft tunnel and one-and-a-half ton blast doors, with space for 600 key government and military personnel complete with a BBC studio and a mortuary. Since 1992, when it was bought by a local farmer, it could be described as the most all-weather tourist attraction in Britain.

A traditional African tribal village has been established at Takeley, near Stansted, to promote African culture. The village, Aklowa, and its variety of Ghanaian huts represent the only organisation of its type in Europe.

The medieval barn housing the Corbett Theatre in Loughton (named after Harry H. Corbett, a benefactor and workshop member) was moved to its site from Ditchling in Sussex in the 1960s. It was dismantled and transported a distance of some 80 miles, and now forms the East 15 campus theatre, part of the University of Essex.

The largest public collection of Latin American art in Europe is in the University of Essex in Colchester, and the largest collection of written material on jazz in the UK is stored at Loughton Library as the National Jazz Archive.

SOME ECCENTRIC VILLAGE NAMES IN ESSEX

Bacon End, originating from Beacon End, the site of a fire beacon.

Chignall Smealey, from Cica's halh (chicken corner) and smethe leah (smooth clearing).

Cock Clarks, associated with John Coke.

Cripple Corner, hazy origins.

Fiddlers Hamlet, originating from the Merry Fiddlers Inn.

Gore Pit, from gore meaning filth and pytt meaning (Old English) well.

Maggots End, possible links to Magot(e) family.

Matching Tye, probably reference to Maecca's people (Matching) and a cross-roads or clearing (Tye).

Mucking, meaning Mucca's people.

Shellow Bowells, from the manor of Scheuele and the manor-owners the (French?) de Bueles or Bouelles.

Ugley, possibly from Ugga's leigh or enclosure.

Wendens Ambo, from ambo meaning both. Used when Great and Little Ambo became one in 1661.

AND SOME ECCENTRIC STREET NAMES

Barnaby Rudge, Chelmsford. (One of a number of streets with a Dickens connection, including Little Nell, Magwitch Close and Quilp Drive).

Break Egg Hill, Billericay, and Burnt Dick Hill, Boxted. Use your imagination for these.

Caracalla Way, Colchester, is one of several streets named after Roman notables, such as Tiberius Crescent, and Maximus Drive.

Cringle Lock, South Woodham Ferrers. A cringle is a small hole in the edge of a sail for passing the rope through.

The Dismals, Terling and Fell Christy, Chelmsford. The Dismals may have gained its name from its location at a crossroads (often associated with the supernatural and the unlucky), and Fell Christy was a partner in a local engineering works making agricultural machinery.

Gandalfs Ride, South Woodham Ferrers. This is one of a number of streets in an area known as the Middle Earth Estate, all with names derived from the Lord of the Rings trilogy. Other examples are Butterbur Chase, Elronds Rest, Hobbiton Hill, and The Withywindle.

Neil Armstrong Way, Leigh-on-Sea, is among a collection of similar names on the Astronaut Estate.

Toot Hill Road, near Chipping Ongar, means a look-out place.

Twitty Fee, Chelmsford, with possible links to William Twitye. Feot is an old name for possession.

TEN ESSEX PLACE NAMES YOU CAN FIND IN THE USA

There is a Braintree in Vermont, a Brentwood in New Hampshire, a Chelmsford in Massachusetts, Colchester(s) in Connecticut and Vermont, Epping in New Hampshire, Harwich in Massachusetts, Romford in Connecticut, Springfield(s) in abundance (with the added status of being home to *The Simpsons*), Wickford in Washington County and Woodford in Vermont.

A FEW ROMAN REMAINS

Colchester still has long stretches of Roman town wall, and the largest, most complete surviving Roman gateway in Britain: the Balkerne Gate. When Camulodunum (as it was known) was developed by the Romans in about AD 43, it was the first time bricks and mortar were used in Britain, creating familiar structures. A giant circus, or chariot racing track, was excavated in the town in Abbey Field in 2004. The circus is the only one to have been found in the UK and one of only six in the world.

ROMAN IN-WADERS LANDING ON THE HARD, WEST MERSEA. WELCOME BY THE NATIVES.
A drawing by the late Sir Francis Carruthers Gould, commemorating a visit to West Mersea, c. 1895, with a party of Essex friends.

A Roman farmhouse and barn at Boreham, near Caesaromagnus (Chelmsford – the only town to be dignified with the imperial title), excavated at the end of last century, produced evidence of an affluent lifestyle such as a bath-house, with signs of such imported food as olives. The site also seems to have been a location for the pursuit of falconry, one of the earliest indicators in Britain of this rich man's pursuit.

A 2m stretch of wall is all that remains of Othona Fort, Bradwell-on-Sea. It was originally a hugely significant defence against the Saxons, built in the later years of occupation (between AD 250 and AD 270) as part of a chain of forts.

The foundations of a Romano-Celtic temple were discovered in Harlow in the 1950s. This square temple features 3ft thick walls, and is one of only fifteen or so known such buildings in Britain, and the only one fronted by a substantial rectangular porch. Six villas and other settlements have also been discovered in the nearby Stort Valley.

Unusual Listed Buildings

Barking Magistrates' Court (built in 1893) – not only the building, but also its railings, lamps and lamp holders.

Renowned for its Art Deco interior is the Baggage Hall at Tilbury Riverside station.

Jetty No. 4 (and the Approach), a 500ft long stretch of jetty in Dagenham Dock, is among Britain's earliest surviving reinforced concrete structures.

The canteen at the Rhône-Poulenc building in Dagenham. This is a post-Second World War edifice, with Rhône-Poulenc since reborn as Aventis Pharma (a pharmaceutical company).

The booking hall concourse at Barking station, opened by the Queen in 1961. Its cantilevered structure was a pioneering design at the time.

Brooke House in Basildon, a 1960s multi-storey tower of flats. This was designed by Sir Basil Spence, architect of Coventry Cathedral.

The Smallest, Largest, Oldest, Longest, Highest

When the Becontree council housing estate (spread over Barking, Ilford and Dagenham) was built in the 1920s, it was the largest council estate in the world. By the time it was completed in 1938, it accommodated 115,652 people in 25,736 dwellings – effectively the first English 'New Town'.

Southend Pier, at 1.33 miles, remains the longest in the world.

Chelmsford was the first place in Britain to install electric street lighting in 1888. However, the council were not forward thinking about such technology and reverted for a while back to gas lighting because it was cheaper.

"The Fishermen down front"

The first purpose-built cinema in the country is reputed to be the Harwich Electric Palace, which has been restored and still attracts cinema-goers. In its original form, from 1911, it attracted fishermen straight from port-side and as a result was sprayed with disinfectant perfume at the end of performances.

The first cinema built after the Second World War was the Odeon in Harlow, opened in 1960.

The highest point of the county is Chrishall Common near the village of Langley, reaching 482ft. At the other extreme, the whole of Canvey Island is lower than high water level.

Cliff Richard made his first professional appearance at Butlins holiday camp in Clacton-on Sea in 1958. The camp was demolished in the 1980s to make way for housing.

A seventeenth-century Dutch cottage in Crown Hill, Rayleigh, is Britain's oldest council house. It is part of the Dutch heritage prevalent in the south of Essex, and is unusually circular and very small.

Manningtree, a once busy port at the head of the Stour Estuary upstream from Harwich, is the smallest town in England.

When the residential towers were built at the Colchester University campus, they were Europe's tallest load-bearing brick structures. They remain the tallest brick buildings in the country.

Essex is home to Great Britain's first capital city, established by the Romans nearly 2,000 years ago, Colchester, which is also Britain's oldest recorded town.

Brentwood was the first town in Britain to install CCTV, in 1994.

The Iron Age settlement discovered at Uphall, near Ilford, is the largest site of its kind in Essex, covering 24 hectares.

Great Bentley is proud of laying claim to having the largest village green in Essex (if not England) at a whopping 42 acres.

Perhaps the oldest surviving timber-framed barn in Europe is Coggeshall Grange Barn, Grange Hill, Colchester, dating from possibly as early as 1140. However, Brightlingsea makes a claim that Jacob's Hall, in the town centre, is the oldest (fourteenth-century) timber-framed building in England. Superseding both, the Barley Barn at Cressing Temple (between Braintree and Witham) describes itself as the oldest timber-framed barn in the world, dating back to 1206. Fyfield Hall (Ongar) has a slightly different claim: to be the oldest 'continually inhabited' timber-framed house in Britain, evidenced by some of its roof timbers having been felled in the twelfth century. Only super sleuths will be able to sort this one out!

Colchester boasts the largest surviving Victorian water tower in Britain (known as Jumbo) at 110ft high. It was named by the local rector (who lived just a few feet from the tower) after an elephant in London Zoo.

Layer Marney Tower (near Colchester) is England's tallest gatehouse, dating from the Tudor period.

At Theydon Garnon is the oldest surviving milestone in the county. It is not very prepossessing, thanks to its proximity to a busy road and to nearby hedges (those hedge cutters can be lethal).

At Rivers Hall, Boxted, you can find what started out as the longest barn in Essex. It was 136ft long when it was built, but lost 64ft in the 1987 storms.

The oldest windmill in Essex is at Great Bardfield. It was built as a prototype brick windmill as early as 1660, because storms were capable of blowing over wooden windmills. It is said to be the first brick tower mill, modelled on a smock mill, and is now a private dwelling.

At 263 hectares, the largest landfill site in Essex is at Mucking. It is due to close in 2010 and be restored as a country park.

When it was built, Audley End House, Saffron Walden, was the largest house in England. It remains the last of the great Essex courtyard houses. It was built in 1614 for the Lord Treasurer, Thomas Howard, and when James I visited during the construction he is said to have reported that it was 'too much for a King but may do for a Lord High Treasurer.'

'The Lawn' in Harlow is the first tower block built in Britain (1951).

Built in 1809, Rayleigh Tower Mill is the highest remaining mill in Essex. It stands 68ft tall and was originally used to grind corn from surrounding areas.

The smallest cottage in East Anglia is a thatched dwelling overlooking the River Stort in Clavering – at just 10ft by 8ft. Chestnut Cottage was built for the ford keeper and needed a ladder to reach the upstairs.

The Maldon mint was the first to operate in Essex, although it is unclear how much earlier it is than the Colchester mint of 991.

Essex Extravagances

The 1679 inventory of Copped Hall (Epping) included, in its 103 rooms, some 250 chairs, 150 stools, 69 tables, 170 tapestries, 50 bedsteads and 16 'bucks' heads'.

Wanstead House, built in 1722 at a cost of £360,000 for Sir Richard Child, had garden and parkland amounting to 300 acres. The elaborate landscaping – an island on one of the lakes was said to represent Great Britain – was such that crowds of people turned up to peer, open-mouthed, at the sight.

The wealthy Richard Rigby, in 1776, hired Robert Adam (the famous architect responsible for such gems as Portland Place and Luton Hoo) to enhance Mistley church with twin towers – these remain, although the church is long gone. Rigby had also planned a saltwater bath, by the river, but this plan was never brought to fruition. Adam's work also survives in the lodges of Mistley Hall, the Rigby family home, but this was the only work he did in Essex.

Bits of London in Essex

The 100ft maypole in The Strand, used by London revellers since the Restoration, was moved, with the assistance of one Isaac Newton, to Wanstead in 1718. His friend, Dr Proud, a curate, needed something on which to place what was the (then) largest telescope in Europe, at some 125ft long. The maypole was replaced by the church of St Mary le Strand, and the telescope provided final proof for Dr Proud that the earth did indeed move around the sun.

When the old London Bridge was removed (in about 1824), the balustrade was taken to Gilwell Park near Epping Forest and could still be seen 140 years later on the front lawn of the Scouts' headquarters at Gilwell. Some of the stones from the bridge were used to construct Beaumont Quay, near Thorpe-le-Soken, and a tablet remains on an old barn recording the event.

St Peter's Church at Aldborough Hatch, completed in 1863, was built mainly of stone from the first Westminster Bridge, demolished in 1861. It is named after the Collegiate Church of St Peter, i.e. Westminster Abbey.

Parts of the London house which William Wilberforce (the abolitionist) used as a weekend retreat were rescued when the Battersea house was demolished and were used in the erection of a holiday bungalow on Canvey Island ('The Settlement'). Doors, windows and decorated wood panels were all successfully salvaged.

Two slender fluted Corinthian columns were erected by Sir Frederick Gibberd (the architect of Harlow New Town) in his garden at Harlow. Apparently, they are relics of Soane's Bank of England which were not wanted after improvements in the 1920s – they were brought to Essex by Gibberd in the 1950s. Gibberd, incidentally, was the designer of Heathrow Airport and the Regent's Park Mosque, and the only New Town designer to live in the town that he had planned.

HALF A DOZEN CASTLES AROUND THE COUNTY

Colchester Castle (Norman) was built on the site of a Roman Temple from re-used Roman materials. It is renowned for having the largest Norman keep in Europe – considerably larger than the White Tower of London – and is still a prominent feature in the town.

Hadleigh Castle was one of the last Norman castles to be built (in about 1230) to stop French invaders, although it never fulfilled its brief. The ruins were the subject of one of Constable's most famous paintings and remain little changed and freely accessible.

Hedingham Castle, North of Colchester, has the largest Norman arch in Europe at 28ft wide and 20ft high, supported on pillars in the second-floor banqueting room. Its 100ft-high keep is said to be the best preserved of its kind in England. (Incidentally, Castle Hedingham is the only town in Essex to have 'Castle' in its name).

Mountfitchet Castle, Stansted (Norman, possibly Saxon), is now the only reconstructed ring and bailey castle in Britain open to visitors.

Pleshey Castle, home of the murdered Thomas Woodstock, Duke of Gloucester (in the fourteenth century), remains as a preserved motte and bailey earthworks. The outer bailey dates from the twelfth century, and used to enclose the whole village.

Rayleigh Castle (Norman), is the only one in Essex referred to in the Domesday Book. Its earthworks remain in the 2 acres of Rayleigh Mount, a small park.

LOCATION, LOCATION, LOCATION:
ON THE BIG SCREEN . . .

Purfleet, at the beginning of the twentieth century, used its former chalk pits to good effect as the backdrop of numerous silent westerns while soldiers from the local barracks played cowboys or Indians as needed. Thurrock had a starring role as far back as the 1928 film *The Guns of Loos*, with locals used as extras. Epping Forest and Upminster both feature in *Full Metal Jacket* (1987). *The Big Sleep* has a scene filmed at The Grotto in Wanstead Park. Tilbury Docks turns up in *Up the Creek* (1958), *Brannigan* (1976) and *The Battle of Britain* (1969) which also features North Weald Airfield. Tilbury's Coalhouse Fort earned £30,000 for its part in *Batman*

Begins (2005) while the Art Deco State cinema in Grays made an appearance not only in *Who Framed Roger Rabbit?* (1988) but also in *Chicago Joe and the Show Girl* (1990). Stansted Airport can be seen in the films *Golden Eye* (1995), *Bridget Jones' Diary* (2001) and *Wimbledon* (2004). *The Fourth Protocol* (1987) was filmed in Colchester and Chelmsford (car chase takes place in the latter), with Colchester also featuring in *Vanity Fair* (2004). *Four Weddings and a Funeral* (1994) has scenes shot at St Clement's Church, West Thurrock, and Tilbury was used as Venice for *Indiana Jones and the Last Crusade* (1989)! In 2002, *28 Days Later* was partly filmed at the Broadview Transport Café near Stanford-le-Hope, at Stansted Airport and North Weald Airfield. Wallasea Island can be seen in *Children of Men* (2006), Clacton Pier in *Kinky Boots* (2005), and Southend Airport in *The Queen* (2006).

. . . AND THE SMALL SCREEN

Lovejoy incorporated many Essex locations including Braintree, Finchingfield, Layer Marney Tower, Maldon, Saffron Walden, Thaxted and Ingatestone Hall. The hall was also a location in the 2005 production of *Bleak House* as well as the setting in *Lady Audley's Secret*. Chelmsford was the location for 1990s *The Chief* police series, and used in the filming of the earlier *Porridge*. *Hi-de-Hi* was filmed at Dovercourt, and *Ivanhoe* – in part – at Hedingham Castle. Southend-on-Sea, Leigh-on-Sea and Clacton-on-Sea have all been seen in *Eastenders*. The Epping Ongar Railway featured in a *Waking the Dead* episode, and the Halfway House pub (Southend arterial) was in an episode of *Z-Cars*. *Dr Who* and *Quatermass* have made good use of the Thurrock chalk pits, and the location for some of *Softly, Softly* was North Ockendon. The later 1980s *Birds of a Feather,* based in Chigwell, could be partly responsible for the Essex girls' reputation. St Osyth's Priory was the setting in P.D. James' *Death in Holy Orders* (2001). Basildon was prominent in *Can't Buy Me Love* (2004), as was Leigh-on-Sea in *Class of '76* (2005). Stansted Airport has been a popular location, appearing in *Cracker, Hustle, Jonathan Creek, Spooks, Man and Boy* (2002), and *Life Begins*. Southend-on-Sea was part of the backdrop in a *London's Burning* episode, its pier can be seen in the credits of *Minder*, and its renowned Kursaal can be seen in *The Avengers,*

The Prisoner, and *Nearest and Dearest.* One episode of *Spooks* was filmed at Bradwell-on-Sea (at the former power station) and another at Theydon Mount, near Epping. *Randall and Hopkirk (Deceased)* also featured episodes in different Epping locations, as did *Murphy's Law.* Wivenhoe gets a look in – in *Plotlands* (1997) and *A Perfect Place* – and Tilbury Docks turns up again in *Murphy's Law.*

A Selection of Lesser-known Museums

Battlesbridge Motor Cycle Museum is likely to be the smallest museum in Essex – or even further afield.

Brentwood Museum, Cemetery Lodge, is sited in a graveyard, perhaps the only one in such a location.

Brewery Chapel Museum, Halstead, is on the site of a brewery which had a chapel installed in the grounds in 1883 for the benefit of those connected with the brewery.

British Postal Museum, Loughton, incorporates not just the history of the British postal service but includes such objects as the desk of Rowland Hill, founder of the Penny Post.

Combined Military Services Museum in Maldon boasts many exhibits from the Cold War. Espionage equipment used by spies on all sides are housed here, the sort of thing that James Bond would relish such as secret cameras, hollowed-out logs and even the typewriter used by the Krogers, KGB spies who posed as London booksellers during the 1960s.

East England Tank Museum, Clacton, specialises in restoring, preserving, and exhibiting historic military vehicles from all over the world.

Essex Aviation Museum at Brightlingsea is housed in a Martello Tower which still boasts its wartime camouflage paint and is still in a position to monitor the detonations from Foulness. Exhibits here include the only George III cannon in East Anglia and a mammoth bone believed to be about 10,000 years old.

Harwich's Maritime and Lifeboat Museums are in a former 1818 lighthouse.

House on the Hill Toy Museum at Stansted Mountfitchet is the largest privately owned toy museum in Europe.

Maeldune Heritage Centre, Maldon, is home to the Maldon Embroidery depicting a thousand years of the town's history; Bayeux eat your heart out.

Mangapps Railway Museum, Burnham-on-Crouch, has a large collection of artefacts, inside and out, plus railway carriages, signal-boxes and the largest railway signalling collection on public display in Britain.

Motorboat Museum, Wat Tyler Country Park, Basildon, is the only museum in the world devoted to the history of motor boats.

Museum of Power, Langford Maldon, is housed in the former 1920s Southend Waterworks Pumping Station. It demonstrates working examples of all power sources.

Paycocke's (National Trust), Coggeshall, Colchester, is a timbered merchant's house dating from about 1500, with domestic Tudor architecture. There is also a display of the locally renowned Coggeshall lace.

Prittlewell Priory Museum, based in a twelfth-century Cluniac Priory, houses an extensive collection of early twentieth-century radios and televisions.

Purfleet Heritage and Military Centre incorporates the Hornchurch Wing Collection and a large collection of RAF memorabilia and artefacts. The centre is housed in the last remaining Royal Gunpowder Magazine of its kind, built in 1759 to hold over 10,000 barrels of gunpowder.

Royal Gunpowder Mills at Waltham Abbey (English Heritage) contains Newton's Pool which was used for the testing of underwater explosives including the explosive used in the famous bouncing bomb.

The site (175 acres in all) also incorporates The Press House, where gunpowder was riskily pressed to improve its explosive properties.

Saffron Walden Museum specialises in ethnography and the study of international cultures, so exhibits include such unexpected Essex treasures as 1820s wooden figures carved in . . . Tahiti.

Thames Sailing Barge (*Glenway*) and Heritage Centre can be found at The Hythe, Maldon. *Glenway* was launched in 1913, one of a fleet of over 2,000 Thames barges, but is one of only a handful still afloat.

Valence House Museum is unusual in that it is housed in the only surviving manor house in Dagenham, dating back to the thirteenth century and partially surrounded by a moat.

Warners Mill Archive at Braintree houses 60,000 fabric samples, 2,500 of which are hand-woven and dating from the 1820s. One of the flywheels, weighing more than ten tons, is preserved in the reception area.

2
BATTLES AND WARS

AD 61: She may have been a warrior queen, but Boudicca is reputed to have committed suicide, not by the sword, but by eating poisonous berries on the banks of Cobbins Brook in Epping Forest.

893: Haesten the Black was a nasty piece of Viking work, so the canny Wessex army (led by Edward, son of Alfred the Great) waited for him to absent himself from his Benfleet camp before they overpowered his men, and burned his ships. Imagine his face upon his return.

991: Beorthtnoth, an Anglo-Saxon nobleman from Essex, led a defensive force against the Vikings and cornered them on Northey Island, leaving them no way of escape. Naïvely, however, he conceded to the Vikings' suggestion for a 'fair' battle (the Battle of Maldon) on open ground, with the result that Beorthtnoth was killed, together with his crack troops.

1016: The Battle of Assandune (either fought near Ashingdon, close to the River Crouch with its easy access for invaders, or at Ashdon in North Essex, depending on which historian you favour) saw the Vikings in action again. This time, Canute fought off Edmund Ironside, becoming the first Viking King of England as a result.

BRAVE HEARTS AND WHITE HARTS

The first attempt of common man to assert his rights did not go according to plan when 20,000 peasants, mainly from Essex, marched on London to confront the juvenile King Richard in 1381 following the introduction of yet another poll tax. They were told there would be no recriminations for their violence en route. Those from Fobbing and elsewhere were obviously too easily fobbed off, because hundreds were slaughtered. The royal troops responsible were commanded by Richard's uncle, Thomas of Woodstock, in the Battle of Billericay at Norsey Woods. Others were killed at Rettendon, another wooded area where the rebels had attempted to hide. King Richard's symbol was a white hart; hence the subsequent number of White Hart public houses in Essex and Kent on the route of the Peasants' Revolt to London.

ROYALISTS AND ROUNDHEADS

During the first Civil War, Essex was not really actively involved because of its universal support for Parliament. However, in the second (in 1648) there was a resurgence in favour of the king. Result: armed conflict, culminating in the Siege of Colchester with the surrender of the Royalists and the shooting of brave local dignitaries. A grim reminder lived on in a clock face on a large house at Little Burstead, the hands of which were said to have been made from the bones of one of the many who had lost his life during the local skirmishes. The bones at Clock House seem to have been since replaced with sheep bones.

The Sun Inn, Church Street, Saffron Walden, was Oliver Cromwell's headquarters in the Civil War.

When St Mary's Church (Colchester) came under siege in 1648, a giant cannon perched on top of the spire was shot to the ground, shattering into several pieces. The King's Men (the Royalists) couldn't put it together again, hence the origins of Humpty Dumpty. But what an interesting place for a cannon.

THE LAST ARMED INVASION OF ESSEX

This came in 1724 from an unexpected source – Kent! One hundred fishing smacks invaded the oyster beds of Leigh-on-Sea, using gunfire when the local fishermen attempted to drive them off. The invaders made off with 1,000 bushels of oysters but were duly apprehended, tried and fined £2,000.

SOME EFFECTS OF THE NAPOLEONIC AND CRIMEAN WARS

Under threat of Napoleonic invasion, a nautical Home Guard was in operation known as the Essex Sea Fencibles. The Home Guard were part-time volunteers, but the one shilling per day expenses they were paid was actually a generous sum. In command (1798–9) was Chigwell man Sir Eliab Harvey, later Captain of the *Temeraire* at the Battle of Trafalgar (1805) and one of the pallbearers at Lord Nelson's funeral.

Tower A on Point Clear (St Osyth) was the first of the chain of Martello Towers built as forts from 1805 along the coast of south-east England to thwart Napoleon's invasion plans – they were re-commissioned 100 years later to keep Hitler at bay. Six are still standing in Essex.

When the Cameron Highlanders were based at Weeley (Clacton Beach) during the Napoleonic Wars, Alexander Mcdonald was attacked and killed by local villagers in a drunken brawl (26 July 1806) and buried in Weeley churchyard. All the accused villagers were acquitted because of unreliable and conflicting evidence.

The Waterloo Road housing estate in Romford was built on the site of the Napoleonic cavalry barracks where soldiers were stationed to defend the capital.

When Private Nehemiah Eastoe returned from the Crimean War (a participant in the Charge of the Light Brigade) he ended up in West Ham Workhouse (East London) with his wife and three children until the Rector of Wanstead came to his rescue. As a result, Nehemiah took on the running of a coffee tavern in Wanstead High Street named, appropriately, The Balaclava.

The prefabricated wooden huts built for Belgian mercenaries at Colchester during the Crimean War were still providing temporary accommodation as infantry barracks until the twentieth century.

THE MACHINE BREAKERS' RIOT 1830–1

At a time when technology was less welcome because of its threat to job security, Little Clacton and surrounding villages (Tendring, Kirby, Great Holland *et al*) were at the centre of the riots led by Captain Swing. Agricultural labourers set to burning ricks and breaking machines, joined by others in Suffolk and further afield. The local statistics are: 23 Essex rioters indicted, 31 acquitted, 69 imprisoned with hard labour, and 23 transported to Van Diemen's Land (now Tasmania). A number of the latter received free pardons in 1835 but most stayed in Oz seemingly preferring the tough life and the mosquitoes.

THE UNLUCKY ESSEX REGIMENT

The 44th Foot, later the Essex Regiment (now the Royal Anglian), has been wiped out not just once but three times; at Prestonpans on 21 September 1745 by the highlanders of Prince Charles Edward Stuart, on 9 July 1755 at Monongahela River in Pennsylvania by the Indians, and in August 1840 at Gandamak in the Afghan Mountains by the Afghans.

SOME ESSEX HOLDERS OF THE VICTORIA CROSS

Field Marshal Sir Henry Evelyn Wood was born in Essex. He was mentioned in dispatches when a midshipman in the Crimean War, and, after switching to the Army, saw action in India at the time of the mutiny during which he was awarded his accolade. He also served during the First Boer War and went on to command the British Army in Egypt. He was buried at Cressing in 1919.

During the Crimean War, another VC was awarded to William Hope from Dagenham. On 18 June 1855 he rescued two wounded soldiers while under fire from the Russians, running across open land with a stretcher.

Edmund Fowler, for some years landlord of the Live and Let Live public house in Stanwell Street, Colchester, was a private in the British Army during the 1879 Zulu Wars. He and his lieutenant cleared the enemy from a narrow path although their captain had been killed.

Private David (Frederick) Corbett, born 1853 at Maldon, remained in the open with a mortally wounded officer under enemy fire at Kafra Dowar in Egypt on 5 August 1882, subsequently helping to carry the lieutenant off the field. He sold his medal on his return to 'civvy street' and died in the Maldon workhouse 25 September 1912. Although buried in an unmarked grave, a 2004 memorial service held by the Commonwealth War Graves Commission unveiled a new headstone to his memory – better late than never.

The Revd Noel Mellish became vicar at St Mary's Church in Dunmow in 1928 after facing enemy fire seventeen times to rescue twenty-two men during the First World War. He stayed at Dunmow, unrecognised, for twenty years, but a plaque was finally dedicated in his honour in 2008 thanks to the Dunmow Historical & Literary Society.

The first success against the German airships took place on the night of 2/3 September 1916 when a night-fighter flown by Lieutenant William Leefe Robinson, flying from Sutton's Farm, Hornchurch, intercepted and shot down a zeppelin, which resulted not only in a Victoria Cross but in £4,200 donated by a grateful public.

Sergeant Laurence Calvert, Dagenham resident, single-handedly captured two machine guns and killed their crews at Havrincourt on 12 September 1918. For this act of bravery, he too was awarded the Victoria Cross.

Sidney Godley, former resident of Torrington Drive, Loughton, was the first private to be awarded the Victoria Cross in the First World War. Godley defended Nimy railway bridge over the River Marne alone when his commander was wounded, in spite of serious gunshot wounds including a bullet in his skull. He was a POW until 1918, and presented with the VC a year later.

Royal Artillery man Lance-Corporal John Sayer (from Chadwell Heath) was awarded for acting on his own initiative and without assistance when fighting off a series of flank attacks in Le Verguier (1918), inflicting heavy casualties on the Germans. He killed many of the enemy and wounded others even though he was subjected to attacks by rifle and machine-gun fire, bombs and bayonets, showing complete contempt for danger the whole time. Sayer held the post until nearly all the garrison had been killed, wounded or captured, although he too had been wounded. He later died of his wounds.

Lieutenant-Colonel Augustus Charles Newman from Buckhurst Hill led the charge to destroy the dock installations of the German-controlled naval base at St Nazaire in March 1942 while under enemy fire. He spent the remainder of the war as a POW.

Sir Tasker Watkins (1918–2007) was partly educated in Romford, and worked in Dagenham until being called up during the Second World War. In 1944, as a lieutenant in Normandy, his battalion crossed open cornfields set with booby traps to attack the enemy. He headed an effective bayonet charge, and, although outnumbered, ordered his men to scatter so that he could charge and silence the enemy at close range. He was actually Welsh, one of only two Welsh soldiers to earn the VC during the Second World War. The pinnacle of his subsequent career was as the Lord Justice of Appeal, and he earned many additional accolades.

THE FIRST WORLD WAR, ESSEX STYLE

Although Tilbury Fort was built to protect the approach to London in the seventeenth century – and remains as the best surviving example of that century's military engineering in England – it did not see action until the twentieth century. Its anti-aircraft guns shot down a zeppelin in the First World War.

The first military aircraft to be based in Essex were the seventy-four tractor sea-planes that landed on West Beach, Clacton, in August 1914 to form a Royal Naval Air Service sub-station – in the same month that Great Britain declared war on Germany. The first RNAS landing ground in Essex opened at Hainault Farm two months later, the 60 acres having been requisitioned. The largest RNAS station in Essex was the 150 acres at Chingford towards the end of 1914.

The first British pilot to intercept an enemy airship over Britain was Lieutenant John Slessor, aged eighteen, on his first operational patrol from Sutton's Farm at Hornchurch (newly requisitioned by the Royal Flying Corps, later the RAF) 13 October 1915.

The first shots at sea during the First World War were fired by the *Lance* off Harwich on 5 August 1914, destroying the SS *Königin Luise*, a German mine-layer. However, the Germans had done their job, because the next day one of the Harwich Force hit one of the mines already laid – fortunately, all the crew survived.

Cars full of Londoners descended on the little village of Great Burstead, near Billericay, in September 1916 to view the wreckage of a zeppelin that had been shot down. Hordes of local people arrived on foot and by pedal power, *The Times* reporting 'hundreds of bicycles' laying abandoned on the fields. Even lemonade sellers set up stalls to profit from the spectators who scoured nearby fields looking for precious debris. Parts of this *L32* still turn up occasionally on eBay. The *L33* suffered a similar fate at New Hall Farm, Little Wigborough, but the crew survived and were taken to a POW camp, and the military did a better job of guarding the wreckage.

Agatha Christie's husband, Malcolm, was the Colonel in Command of 49 Wing at Sutton's Farm Airfield in 1918.

The lock-up at Bradwell-on-Sea was the last to be used for its official purpose during the First World War when a 'suspicious-looking' foreigner was incarcerated.

Edwin Dunning, DSC, from Bradfield, Manningtree, lost his life when demonstrating 'how to land an aeroplane on the deck of a Man of War while it was moving.' After two successful landings, obtaining data indispensable to any fleet, his third ended in his death.

The Essex Regiment provided thirty infantry battalions during the First World War, and lost 9,000 men in the fighting. A rifle originally issued to the 1st Essex Regiment was carried by T.E. Lawrence (Lawrence of Arabia) during the Arab Revolt. This rifle is now at the Imperial War Museum at Duxford, and sports five notches cut in the stock to denote the number of Turks shot by Lawrence.

Chelmsford Gaol was used exclusively for military prisoners and POWs for the duration of the First World War.

The most comfortable billet in the RAF during the First World War, according to the earliest British pilots, was at Rochford, then the largest aerodrome in Essex. Not for long, however, because the area reverted to farmland at the end of the war until required again at a later date.

An escaped German POW, Gunther Plüschow, managed to smuggle himself onto the Dutch steamer, *Micklenberg*, when it set sail from Tilbury in July 1915. Kaiser Wilhelm II was so impressed by Gunther's successful escape from an internment camp that he was rewarded with the Iron Cross, First Class.

Osea Island was used as a naval base during the First World War with 2,000 ratings being stationed there. It was also a secret base for motor torpedo boats.

In 1914, Millican Dalton, a mountaineer who lived at Hale End, near Woodford, kept up his skill by climbing trees in Epping Forest.

Unfortunately for him, he was spotted in the branches, and arrested as a German spy. Luckily he had enough friends locally to convince the Woodford magistrates of the truth of his unlikely tale.

So many members of the armed forces were billeted in Colchester garrison (20,000 by September 1914, and 40,000 eventually) that not only houses but local warehouses were requisitioned. Even tents and every type of wooden hut were used as additional accommodation.

The longest surviving British cavalryman from the First World War period was Albert Marshall, born at Elmstead Market, who died in 2005 at the ripe old age of 108.

Two non-combatants executed by the Germans are remembered in Essex. There is a memorial to Nurse Cavell (shot 12 October 1915) in Steeple Bumpstead church, recalling her attempts to help Belgian, French and British soldiers to escape from the Germans. Similarly, Captain Charles Algernon Fryatt (shot 27 July 1916) has a memorial at Dovercourt, a reminder of his bravery when ramming German U-boats to prevent their attacking his steamship.

There is a house oddly named Abuka in Tiptree, gaining its name from the HMS *Abuka* on which the house's owner, Charlie Moss, served in the First World War.

... AND THE SECOND WORLD WAR

Within a few months, nineteen airfields were built in Essex in preparation for the Second World War, giving a total of twenty-three in operation. The area was ideal; flat, few large centres of population, and offering the shortest route for attacking Germany. For instance, the splendid Easton Lodge at Great Dunmow was requisitioned by the Army and Home Guard, resulting in thousands of estate trees being either felled or blown up to enable its use as an airfield. Each individual airfield required some 130,000 tons of concrete, ballast and cement, and 50 miles of pipe and conduit. Great Dunmow was the first base on General Eisenhower's 1944 itinerary during his USAAF tour. By September 1944, there were over 2,700 airmen and 68 aircraft at Great Dunmow.

Caissons were the hollow concrete bases forming part of the Mulberry Harbours, which you can still see in Normandy. Sections of these were built at Barking and the floating harbour was towed down river, along with different parts made in different areas of the country, enabling the Allied Forces to access the Normandy beaches on D-Day. Broken sections turn up occasionally – one can be seen off Southend-on-Sea, although it is under threat of demolition by the MOD.

The Battle of Barking Creek in September 1939 is the rousing name given to a less than rousing incident – it refers to the night when two Hawker Hurricanes from North Weald Airfield were shot down by Hornchurch pilots when mistaken for the enemy, thanks to a misinterpretation of radar plotting.

The only memorial in Essex to remember an incident of friendly fire is at Walton on the Naze. Three salvaged Halifax propeller blades mark the spot where the Halifax was brought down, killing the mostly-Canadian crew.

There were over 2,800 defence sites in Essex, including pill-boxes, minefield control towers and gun casements. In the Thurrock marshes and other flat areas, poles and wires were spread to prevent enemy gliders or aircraft landing.

The first Second World War civilian deaths by enemy action in the country were at Clacton on 30 April 1940.

The first pilot to die – on 10 July 1940 – in the official Battle of Britain was twenty-two-year-old Sergeant Ian Clenshaw from Southend-on-Sea, after only one year in the RAF volunteer reserves.

The first POWs in Essex arrived in 1941, mainly Italians, and had a camp built for them at Wakering Common.

The first enemy aircraft shot down at night by a fighter aircraft was credited to Flight-Lieutenant 'Sailor' Malan who downed two Heinkel bombers, flying a Hurricane out of Rochford.

The Royal Signal Corps established a pigeon-breeding establishment in 1942 at the Salvation Army Colony in Hadleigh, near Southend-on-Sea. Up to 500 birds at a time were packed in containers and dropped over occupied Europe with messages to and from resistance groups. It is also rumoured that the French Maquis had their own pigeons in cotes alongside The Anchor public house at Hullbridge; the landlord sent messages brought back from France to British Intelligence in London, with the help of the railway guards en route.

The Dagenham Girl Pipers were among the entertainers sent out to Egypt to entertain the troops.

By the end of the Battle of Britain, Hornchurch claimed to have had the top scoring squadron and pilot. 603 Squadron claimed to have destroyed fifty-eight enemy aircraft and Eric Lock from 41 Squadron downed at least twenty.

The oldest pilot to participate in the Battle of Britain was Warrant Officer Ernest 'Tubby' Mayne, aged thirty-nine, based at RAF Hornchurch.

Epping Forest was like a large campsite during the Second World War for refugees who had quit the East End of London.

Six cockle boats from Leigh-on-Sea ferried some 1,000 soldiers apiece in repeated trips from the beaches of Dunkirk to the large ships at anchor in deep water. They were among the little ships evacuating British soldiers in May 1940 in an armada of civilian boats, but one (the *Renown*) hit a mine on the way back and four lives were lost.

Brentwood was an unlucky selection for the 6,000 children evacuated there in 1939 – over 1,000 bombs were dropped on the town during the war. Altogether, 160,000 bombs were dropped on Essex between 1939 and 1945.

At its height, the Essex Home Guard, originally the Essex Local Defence Volunteers, mustered 40,000 men, with 115,000 men and women taking part by 1945.

Over 100 expectant mothers from the East End of London gave birth in the unlikely setting of Danbury Palace, which was utilised as an emergency maternity hospital for them during the war. Its ballroom was the main lying-in ward; and very nice it was too!

Other stately homes had more secret uses – Hylands House near Chelmsford was the headquarters of the SAS, and Audley End was used by the SOE (Special Operations Executive) for training a total of 527 Polish agents in guerrilla warfare.

Frankie Howerd, when stationed as a Royal Artillery gunner at 22 Regiment, Shoeburyness Barracks, in 1939 is remembered not for his

military exploits but for the concerts he gave at the Garrison Theatre and at the Palace Theatre in Westcliff-on-Sea. His *double entendres* nearly ended in his being arrested, but the local padre pleaded his case. It seems, incidentally, that a poster advertising one of these shows mis-spelt his name (originally Howard) and it stuck.

RAF Chigwell was an RAF base without any aeroplanes – no one ever flew from the site, which focused on wartime barrage balloons.

The American Black Death Group (391st Bombardment Wing) took over the aerodrome at Dunmow in 1944. Between them they took part in 6,000 sorties from Matching carrying millions of pounds-worth of high explosive which they dropped on Germany; 197 airmen were lost, missing or killed, and a memorial remains in the church.

Several internment camps were set up in Essex for POWs, e.g. at Romford and at Langdon Hills, but the most unlikely site was the Butlins Holiday Camp at Clacton.

The Lobster Smack on Canvey Island was used as a shore station for the River Emergency Service in 1939. It was known as a stone frigate and was manned by Sea Scouts logging the largest movement of vessels ever known from the Thames Estuary.

The centre of minesweeping operations for the coastline was established at Brightlingsea.

It wasn't just the American GIs that took Essex girls back home as wives during and after the Second World War; about 500 Canadians (who arrived in 1940) did the same.

One of the only four British citizens convicted of high treason after the war was Walter Purdy, a naval lieutenant from Barking and a member of the Ilford branch of the British Union of Fascists. He was sentenced to death in 1945 for distributing SS propaganda leaflets, the sentence being reduced on appeal to life imprisonment – although in the event he only served nine years.

On Boxing Day 1946, Hatfield Heath villagers challenged local POWs (Germans and Italians) to a football match, and lost 11–0.

3

ROYAL ESSEX

SPORTY KINGS

One of King John's favourite hobbies was destroying castles, especially if they were manned by rebels opposing his position. Although he wiped out Stansted Mountfitchet Castle in 1215, he left enough stones behind for the locals to attempt some early recycling by reusing them to build their own, rather smaller, dwellings. Castle Hedingham and Colchester Castle also stood in his way, but he was unable to wipe these off the Essex landscape, not for the want of trying.

The royal family used the forest of Essex for hunting from Edward the Confessor onwards. 'Forest' was originally a legal term denoting land where the monarch could enjoy the right to hunt for pleasure, dating from the time of Canute. Anyone caught poaching the king's deer (particularly, but not only, in the seventeenth century) could be maimed or even executed, although they often escaped with fines. Dogs were kept by Essex foresters (the forest 'police') for defence, and had three claws removed from each front paw to prevent them chasing game. Commoners had to purchase a licence if they wanted to graze cattle or sheep in the forests.

George V raced *Britannia* at Southend-on-Sea during the first Southend Yachting Week in 1921, winning his race and raising the profile of sailing.

FIGHTING KINGS

When Henry IV's ship was attacked by French pirates en route from Sheppey to Leigh-on-Sea (across the Thames) in 1406, he managed to find safe ground on the Strand wharf in Leigh. So thankful was he at his double escape (from the plague in London and the pirates at sea) that he went down on his knees with thanks for his safe delivery.

Henry V's successful battle at Agincourt led him to offer thanks in the form of the tower at Canewdon church. Even now, revellers dance round the base of Henry's Tower at Halloween.

ROYAL EXECUTIONS

George Boleyn, brother of King Henry VIII's wife Anne, held the manor of Fobbing and the stewardship of Rayleigh during the 1530s, and was created Lord Rochford in February 1533. Less happily, he was executed for treason and incest (with Anne) in 1536.

The sound of the gun at the Tower of London could be heard from High Beach at Epping Forest, and this is where King Henry VIII and his followers were said to have waited on the day Anne Boleyn was beheaded. The sound of the gun confirmed that the execution had in fact taken place.

In 1649, Sir Henry Mildmay of Wanstead (now part of Greater London) was one of the judges who condemned King Charles I to his death. The execution took place on 30 January, the king being the first monarch to be put on trial for treason.

ROYAL INTERVENTIONS

In the eleventh century, Edward the Confessor banished nightingales from the royal palace at Havering-atte-Bower because they disturbed his devotions.

A Royal Charter was issued by Henry II in 1171 to enable him to use Maldon's port for his personal trading.

Richard I, anxious to raise money for his crusade, decided that Colchester's oyster fishery would be willing to pay 60 marks for a Royal Charter, but no money eventually changed hands. Instead, the townspeople paid most of the debt off by working on the king's castle.

A new-fangled and expensive addition to Havering Palace was installed by Henry II in 1215: a private bath.

On 6 May, 1882, Queen Victoria visited High Beach (also known as High Beech) to declare Epping Forest open to the public. Half a million people are reputed to have turned up for her visit, most of them from East London.

Between 1 and 6 July 1381, Richard II's manor house at Writtle was the seat of government, identifying rebel leaders following the suppression of the Peasants' Revolt.

In the 1930s, George VI ordered a beach to be created in the shadow of Traitors' Gate at the Tower of London for the use of East End families. The tons of sand to create this beach were shipped in from the Essex coast.

A KING-KILLER FROM ESSEX?

Sir Walter Tyrrell of Langham was out hunting in the New Forest with William II in 1100 when a shot – seemingly aimed at a deer –

ricocheted off a tree and killed the king. Bearing in mind that William was an unpopular ruler, and that he had red hair, there has since been speculation as to whether this may have indeed been a deliberate act, or even that he was mistaken for a squirrel. Hmm. Whatever the truth, Sir Walter did not linger in Langham. Instead, he fled to France, leaving plenty of questions behind.

STRANGE ROYAL EVENTS

The legend lives on that Helena, later St Helena, was the daughter of Coel, King of Essex and Hertfordshire. The story goes that she married, or had an affair with, Constantius Chlorus and had a son called Constantine. King Coel was king of part of England during Celtic times and the name 'Colchester' means Cole's Castle in Latin. It is possible, if a tad improbable, that Colchester was named after this king, familiar from the nursery rhyme. A statue of St Helena, patron saint of Colchester, crowns its town hall.

A fascinating story surfaced in 2007 suggesting that one of the princes believed to have been murdered by their uncle Richard III was allowed to live, under guard, with his mother after the older prince died of natural causes. It has been suggested, and evidenced, that Prince Richard was taken to St John's Abbey at Colchester after being reunited with his mother and that he kept a low profile by working as a bricklayer until 1539 – a very low profile indeed, it seems.

The Prince Imperial, Louis Napoleon (great nephew of Bonaparte), was hailed as the most enthusiastic student at the Shoeburyness School of Gunnery when on a course in 1875. To avoid curious crowds when he arrived at Shoebury, he had travelled third class on the railway and, upon alighting, had joined in the cries of 'Vive the Prince Imperial' in an apparently convincing cockney accent. The crowds could not have been impressed at missing a sighting of the prince.

A Wanstead housewife wearing white gloves was mistaken for the Duchess of York when the car she was in – en route to see the 1926 visit by the Duke (later George VI) and Duchess – turned by mistake into Ilford's Cranbrook Road, duly sanded and flagged in honour of the occasion. Not wanting to disappoint the cheering crowds, she gamely assumed the royal wave. What happened when the real Duchess and Duke arrived is not recorded.

Royal Births and Deaths

The last Anglo-Saxon king, Harold II, was buried on the site of Waltham Abbey after his defeat at the Battle of Hastings in 1066.

Matilda of Boulogne, queen to King Stephen, the last Norman monarch to rule England, died at Hedingham Castle on 3 May 1151 or 1152 (sources disagree).

Robert Bruce, King of Scotland, was born at Montpeliers Farm, Writtle, Chelmsford, on 11 July 1274, although some historians would dispute this.

Joan of Navarre, the second wife of Henry IV (and the first widow to marry an English king), died in 1437 at Pyrgo Palace, Havering-atte-Bower.

Mary Boleyn, sister of Anne and ex-mistress of Henry VIII, died at Rochford Hall in 1543.

Royal Scandals: Legends and Facts

In about 1212, it seems that King John lusted after Matilda Fitzwalter. The young virgin persuaded her father to send her to Dunmow as a nun, but this seems to have angered the king rather than deterred him. According to legend, the result of this rejection was that Matilda, the girl he couldn't have, was poisoned by a royal messenger. Matilda, incidentally, was called Maid Marian by some, yet another source of legend, especially as Dunmow Priory – no longer standing – is alleged to have been the resting place of Robin Hood's Maid Marian. A tomb to Lady Matilda remains in the church.

Princess Beatrice, daughter of King Henry III, is said to have attempted to elope to France with Ralph de Binley, her chosen suitor, from Leigh-on-Sea in about 1255. When boarding the ship they had been awaiting, a foreign merchant challenged them and died in the struggle. The princess was arrested and returned to London and Ralph was imprisoned at Hadleigh Castle, tried at Chelmsford and sentenced to death. King Henry then agreed a royal pardon for Ralph in return for his daughter's promise to marry John of Brittany who was considered more suitable.

Thomas Woodstock, Duke of Gloucester and son of Edward III, the owner of Pleshey Castle (north of Chelmsford), was taken from the castle and murdered in France on the orders of Richard II in 1397. Two years after he was buried at Pleshey, his murderer, John de Holland, was also executed (for the same reason: treason against the king) at Pleshey. Shakespeare immortalised Pleshey in *Richard II* when Richard's wife says to Edmund:

> With all good speed at Plashy [*sic*] visit me. Alack, and what shall good old York there see, But empty lodgings and unfurnished walls, Unpeopled offices, untrodden stones?

ROYAL APPOINTMENTS

William Gilbert (1544–1603) of Tymperleys, Trinity Street, Colchester, was chief physician to Queen Elizabeth I and James I. His father was one of the servants for Henry VIII. William was responsible for discovering the first principles of electro-magnetism, laying the foundation for electricity. He died in London during a plague epidemic but is buried in Holy Trinity Church, Colchester.

Sir George Biddell Airy, who attended Colchester Royal Grammar School (founded by Henry VIII in 1539), was appointed Astronomer Royal in 1835. He was responsible for installing advanced astronomical apparatus at the Royal Observatory in Greenwich, and expanding both staff numbers and their workload.

Queen Elizabeth II's dress designer, Sir Hardy Amies, was the son of Captain Amies, land agent on the Becontree Estate at Dagenham during its construction in the 1920s.

The Queen's organist at St George's Chapel, Windsor, from 1961 was Dr Sidney Campbell from Ilford.

ROYAL RESIDENTS

The Danish King Canute and his wife Emma lived at Canewdon from about 1020 to 1024, after the king's victory at 'Assandun'.

William the Conqueror spent his first New Year in England staying at Barking Abbey, built in 666 and rebuilt in the tenth century after being destroyed by the Vikings.

Havering Palace was part of Queen Eleanor's 'dower' and in 1267 the palace, village and park (some 16,000 acres) became the property of the queens of England, although still known as the King's House and Park at Havering.

Lionel Plantagenet, son of King Edward III, lived at Claret Hall, Ashen in North Essex.

Henry VI's queen, Margaret of Anjou (unpopular with the people and, like all the House of Anjou, considered to be a witch) briefly lived at Pleshey in the 1450s.

Anne Boleyn spent some of her childhood at her grandfather's residence, Rochford Hall, and her sister, Mary, inherited the property on Anne's untimely death.

In 1548, Edward VI allowed the future Queen Mary to live at Copped Hall, where she remained essentially a prisoner due to her Catholicism. She also lived for some time at New Hall, Boreham, and, when danger from Queen Elizabeth I threatened, moved to Woodham Walter with a boat kept ready nearby at Maldon to spirit her away.

Several of the wives of Henry VIII seemed to have taken up temporary residences both at the Royal Manor at Great Bardfield and at Hadleigh Castle. If they lived long enough, that is. Before this, both Edward IV's wife and his mother spent time in Hadleigh Castle – draughty, but with great views over to Kent.

Charles II bought Audley End House at Saffron Walden in 1668, using it as a base for attending Newmarket races in Suffolk, about 18 miles distant. When Sir Christopher Wren warned the later king, William III, that the house needed major repairs, William returned it pretty sharply to its former owners.

Prince Louis Lucien Bonaparte, Napoleon's nephew, lived in Loughton in High Beach during the nineteenth century. He was a noted politician and philologist.

Unwelcome Royals

When John de Vere, Earl of Oxford, entertained Henry VIII at Hedingham Castle, he rather foolishly boasted of his vast retinue of staff. As a result, he was fined 15,000 marks for breaking a law that restricted nobles to a certain number of servants.

Visits from members of the royal family, while flattering, were likely to cause financial hardship to the hosts and hostesses. Queen Elizabeth I, on her progresses through Essex, sent harbingers (forerunners) to check the accommodation and facilities on offer. The high standards she required resulted in the expression harbingers of doom.

On 19 October 1638, Maria de Medici (widow of Henry IV of France) landed at Harwich to visit her son-in-law Charles I – and stayed three years! She favoured the stylish Gidea Hall in Romford above the more spartan Havering Palace.

ROYAL MISTRESSES

There is supposition that Maud de Ingelrica, wife of Ranulph Peverel in the eleventh century – and therefore associated with (and buried in) Hatfield Peverel – was the mistress of William the Conqueror. One of her sons, William, is suggested to have been fathered by the Conqueror. As Maud founded a religious college in the area, which later became a priory, this has been interpreted as atonement for her sins.

Alice Perrers was mistress of King Edward III in the fourteenth century. She lived out her life at her manor in Upminster, but had spent time before that at many of the royal palaces, especially at Havering.

Henry VIII had more mistresses than most – and Elizabeth 'Bessie' Blount became associated with Blackmore after giving birth in the priory there to a baby boy, proving that Henry could indeed sire a son. Her lying-in was arranged by Cardinal Wolsey, and he also arranged a marriage for her soon after. The boy, Henry Fitzroy (Fitzroy means 'sired by a regent') was bestowed with numerous titles by the king, but, sadly, died at the age of seventeen. If he had grown to adulthood and made a claim on the throne, this could have been one king born in Essex. The link remains in the gold crown on the village sign.

Mary Boleyn, with her Rochford associations, was another notch on Henry VIII's bedpost, prior to his involvement with her sister.

The mistress of Frederick Augustus Hanover, Duke of York, from 1803, was Mary Anne Clarke, an actress from Ham (now divided into West Ham and East Ham in East London), and later long-time resident of Loughton Lodge. This enterprising lady threatened to publish a full account of her affair in the manner of a twenty-first-century kiss-and-tell, until suitably financially rewarded.

Edward, Prince of Wales (later Edward VII), turned his attentions from Lillie Langtry to Frances, the Countess of Warwick, whose marital home was Easton Lodge in Great Dunmow. She was to become his 'Darling Daisy' and she too was persuaded not to publish her memoirs, resulting in her debts being mysteriously settled.

The After-Effects of 'The Glorious One'

Queen Elizabeth I, astride her famous white horse, addressed the 23,000 troops encamped at Tilbury in 1588 accompanied by 2,000 horsemen, her famous speech motivating and inflaming men who, in many cases, had no battle experience whatsoever. A shame for them then that the weather and the English seamen were able to deal with the Spanish ships without their needing a single pike, drawn and ready. (The Tudor Rose was subsequently included in Thurrock's coat-of-arms).

During that famous visit, Queen Elizabeth came over tired a couple of times, with interesting local repercussions – at what is now Corbets Tey, it seems she told a member of her staff to 'Stay, Corbet, stay' . . . and at Purfleet, on climbing Beacon Hill, she is reputed to have said 'My poor fleet.' The latter is even less likely, given that the name probably dates back to the thirteenth century – perhaps she said 'my poor feet'?

4

CRIME AND PUNISHMENT

EARLY PENALTIES

In 1279, the penalty for poaching deer, boar or hares in the Royal Forests of Essex was to lose one's eyesight. Hares, incidentally, were designated honorary deer, a delicacy for the rich, the poor having to make do with rabbit.

Dr John Bastwick, born in Writtle in 1593, was a Puritan who refused to recant at the time of Charles I. He was fined £1,000, excommunicated, and imprisoned for abusing the established church in his writings. However, this gave further fuel to his pen, and he continued to write against the tyrannical courts and his wrongful imprisonment. This led to further punishment including the letters SL (for seditious libeller) branded into his cheek in the pillory and, worse, mutilation when both ears were cut off. In 1633, he was sent to the farthest gaol – in the Scilly Isles – and remained there until parliament had the court verdict set aside seven years later. The financial compensation he received could hardly make up for the loss of his hearing.

The body of Captain Kidd, covered in tar, was hung in a metal gibbet for the duration of three high tides at Tilbury Ness in 1699. He had been executed at Execution Dock, East London, but the location of the gibbet was thought to be a deterrent against piracy to other sailors travelling up and down the River Thames.

An advanced form of treadmill was developed by John Richmond of Chelmsford who, in 1823, installed one at the Halstead House of Correction. Treadmills were abolished in 1898.

THE SCAFFOLD IN ESSEX

The only woman to be hanged at Moulsham Gaol, Chelmsford, was Elizabeth Langham in March 1804. She was the wife of a trooper in the 18th Light Dragoons in Colchester, and had murdered her child in her husband's absence.

The last death sentence for sheep-stealing was at Southend-on-Sea in 1820 when two local men were hanged. Thomas Fairhead, a butcher from Rochford, and Henry Gilliot, a shepherd from Prittlewell, were both just twenty-three years old.

The first man to be hanged at Springfield Prison (Chelmsford) was James Winter, alias Reuben Martin, executed 10 December 1827 for the murder of the landlord of the Yorkshire Grey at Colchester. Thomas Patrick, the landlord, was an early example of a have-a-go hero, intervening when Winter attempted to rob another customer, but paying dearly for his action when Winter struck him down. Winter's corpse was hung for the prescribed hour and then cut down and given to the prison surgeon for dissection.

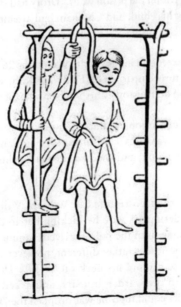

William Calcraft from Great Baddow was Britain's longest surviving hangman. He was born in 1800, the eldest of twelve children, and started work as a hangman aged twenty-nine, continuing in that role for forty-five years. He received one guinea (21s) per week from the Newgate authorities, and a further guinea for each execution, the rate increasing to £10 for each execution outside London, e.g. Chelmsford. It was cheaper for Chelmsford to pay him £10 apiece than employ their own full-time executioner.

The first woman to be executed at Springfield was Mary May, aged thirty-eight, from Wix. She had murdered her brother William, who revelled in the nickname Spratty, in an attempt to benefit from his insurance. This event attracted 3,000 spectators on 14 August 1848, the first execution there for nine years.

Record crowds turned up for the (public) double execution of Thomas Drory and Clavering's Sarah Chesham on 25 March 1851 at Chelmsford. Hawkers, pickpockets and smashers (passers of counterfeit coins) had a field day among the thousands of spectators. The convulsive struggles on the scaffold kept the blood-thirsty crowd entertained for several minutes – but from 1867 their fun was spoiled when executions were conducted within the prison walls. (Drory had strangled the young woman carrying his child, and Chesham had attempted to poison her husband after seeing off several of their children.)

The last public execution in the county was on the 26 January 1865. An immense crowd turned up to see off Ferdinand Kohl, who had murdered Christian Fuhrop on Plaistow Marsh (which was then in Essex).

The first Essex execution conducted in private was that of Michael Campbell, who was convicted of murdering Samuel Galloway at Stratford, East London, and was executed at Chelmsford on 24 April 1871.

A quarrel over tobacco resulted in William Wilkes, a Canewdon shepherd, murdering his wife by kicking her to death. He carried on calmly smoking until the police arrived, summoned by one of his sons. His behaviour was rather different, however, as the executioner placed the noose around his neck on 19 July 1898. It seems that Wilkes turned to the warder, in tears, and asked if it would hurt. Before the warder could reply he was dropped the 7ft 2in to his death.

The last man to be hanged at Chelmsford in the nineteenth century was Samuel Crozier, the landlord of the Admiral Rous. He had beaten his wife regularly in the year that they'd been married, an unfortunate whose maiden name of Savage was far more suited to her husband. The execution took place on 5 December 1898.

The oldest man to be hanged in Britain in the twentieth century was seventy-one-year-old German-born Charles Frembd, who was also the last man to be executed at Springfield on 4 November 1914. He cut his wife's throat (in Leytonstone) and suffered the indignity not just of the execution but of hitting his head on the trap door when he was 'dropped'.

Notorious not Just in Essex

Dick Turpin was reputedly born at The Bell Inn, Hempstead in 1704, his mugging lifestyle since romanticised beyond recognition. He seems to have had hide-outs at Sewardstone and High Beach, frequented The Spotted Dog at Upton, and, as a hobby, raided churches in and around the area, including Chingford and Barking. He is known to have been the ringleader of the Essex Gang for a while before taking off up north to escape the Essex Constabulary.

Captain (or more accurately Colonel) Thomas Blood, the man who tried to steal the Crown Jewels from King Charles II in 1671, was living at an apothecary shop near South Street, Romford, at the time of his crime. He was operating as a respectable physician under the name of Ayliffe and had also used the alias of Weston. Although he nearly succeeded, he was imprisoned for only a few weeks as Charles seems to have admired his impudence, which resulted in his benefiting by a pension of £500 per year.

Matthew Hopkins, known as the Witchfinder General, was not even thirty when he died in 1647, but acquired quite a reputation during his relatively short lifetime. His favourite methods of finding witches included ducking (if she drowned she was innocent, if she lived she was guilty and hanged!), sleep deprivation (resulting in a confession just to get some sleep), and pricking the skin while he searched for the devil's marks e.g. birth-marks, moles, warts, etc. For each one put to

death, he was generously paid and over eighty people, mostly women, mostly old and with prominent facial features, were brought to the gallows in Essex. His record for executions in one day was nineteen. The overall total, bearing in mind that he branched out into Norfolk and Suffolk, too, is difficult to quantify, but was certainly in the hundreds. Hopkins himself, a failed lawyer, lived at Manningtree for a while, although his father was a puritan minister from Suffolk. It's worth bearing in mind that Hopkins had the official blessing of the monarchy and the Pope, and was operating at a time when fear of the supernatural was at its height.

George Smith, the Brides in the Bath murderer from East London, seems to have been more faithful to his Essex 'wife' than any of the others he had 'married' – or she may just have been the only one foolish enough to take him back. Edith Pegler and he purchased a house in Southend-on-Sea before the First World War, coughing up £240 cash (from his ill-gotten gains from an earlier bigamous liaison) and a £30 mortgage. Later, the couple invested in a second-hand furniture shop in the area, but this venture was sold at a loss. Edith was the only woman he married using his real name, one of the last to receive a letter from him before his execution in August 1915 (on unlucky Friday 13th) and the only one who seems to have mourned his death.

MORE ESSEX WITCHERY

Between 1560 and 1700, 229 people were indicted for witchcraft in Essex, compared to 91 in Kent and 17 in Sussex. Between 1560 and 1680, 2,300 people were involved in cases of witchcraft in the county, as suspect or victim. Over 500 of these were prosecuted.

It is said that as long as Canewdon Church tower stands, there will be six witches in the village. Every time a stone falls from the tower, one witch will die and another will take her place. When the last witch dies, the tower will fall. At midnight on Halloween every year those who believe, or those just after a jolly with a difference, congregate to dance 'with the witches'.

THE ERA OF THE HIGHWAYMAN

In the seventeenth century, Frank Osborne, born to a wealthy family in Colchester, was all set on a career as a goldsmith, but lost so much money gambling that he became a highwayman. This turned out to be a short-term, and ineffectual solution to his money worries as he was caught and executed at the age of twenty-nine.

Charles Sackville, the 6th Earl of Dorset, and owner of Copped Hall in Epping from 1674, was tried for manslaughter after being attacked by highwaymen en route from Waltham to London. In the fracas, a tanner called Hoppy was fatally wounded but as his death was obviously a 'mistake', the earl was pardoned and released.

Some of the seventeenth-century hauls were substantial even by today's standards. The Newgate Calendar details a haul of '5000*l*. in gold' en route from Holland and 'belonging to some Jews in London' that was seized from two mail carriers (on horse-back) in April 1686 near Ilford. Two of the three involved were hanged just three months later. A year later, 25 June 1687, a lone highwayman robbed the mail carrier between Harwich and Colchester of £6,750 worth of diamonds.

In 1690, a group of Civil War soldiers who were unable to find lawful employment set themselves up as the Waltham Blacks – so called because they sooted their faces before going out to rob and steal in and around Waltham Abbey. Their leader called himself King Orronoko, and their 'kingdom' encompassed Epping Forest, an ideally secluded arena for highwaymen.

Stephen Bunce would have made a good twenty-first century hustler. Stories include stealing a donkey (with the help of a colleague) from behind an unsuspecting Essex farmer. Stephen sported the bridle over his head when the farmer turned, thinking his donkey had 'turned into' a man. His explanation was that he had been transformed into a donkey for committing a sin, but was a man again now that he had atoned. The stunned farmer, not surprisingly, let him go. Bunce also stole a horse at Romford when the owner saw him with his ear to the ground and handed him the reins so that he, too, could listen to the 'fairy music'! This imaginative rogue was hanged in 1707.

A respectable businessman by day, Gilbert Craddock (or Cutter Lynch) was a highwayman by night. His horse, Brown Meg, was a tad distinctive, however, being without ears. To avoid being easily detected ('look out for the horse with no ears') he had a wax pair made – the perfect disguise. It didn't stop him being tracked down eventually to his home at Lapwater Hall (formerly Leigh Park House), Leigh-on-Sea, in 1751, where his body was discovered in his own pond after he'd been wounded.

The Sixteen String Jack is a pub at Theydon Bois, Epping, named after local highwayman, John (or Jack) Rann who wore eight coloured ribbons fluttering from each knee. He was pretty good at avoiding detection, in spite of attracting attention to himself, as he was accused and acquitted six times before being found guilty and hanged at Tyburn in 1774, aged twenty-four.

Gallows Corner, the major roundabout and flyover at Romford, was once the site of the only double gibbet in Essex where hanged bodies were displayed to deter highwaymen and footpads.

MEN OF CONSCIENCE

William Parker, Lord Monteagle of Great Hallingbury Hall, was the recipient of a letter in 1605 warning of the gunpowder plot. Instead of fleeing from the plotters, he organised a watch in the vaults of parliament which led to their arrest, including Guy Fawkes of course. He was rewarded with land and pension worth £700 per annum.

Henry Nunn, a blacksmith from Coggeshall, was not at all happy about unsightly blots on the Essex landscape – mainly derelict cottages owned by farmers or landowners. So, he took it upon himself to demolish any such eyesores, regardless of their ownership, and quite illegally. As a result, Nunn (who died in 1896) became a local hero in spite of, or because of, spells in prison for his activities.

SMUGGLING HERITAGE

The east of England was ideal for smuggling with its remote beaches, hidden creeks, marshes and problematic tides. Some principal locations include those below.

Paglesham, north of Southend-on-Sea. At one time it seems that the whole population of Paglesham was involved in illegal smuggling, and so much gin was being brought in that they used it to clean their windows. One of the county's most famous smugglers, William Blyth, or Hard Apple, King of the Smugglers, was a Paglesham man. He was a busy fellow, operating as an oyster merchant, village grocer and church warden.

Canvey Island – especially The Lobster Smack public house. From here, Hadleigh Castle can be clearly seen, and was the ideal lookout point to send messages to smugglers.

Mersea Island – the pond alongside the Peldon Rose public house had a large well hidden in the middle, where weighted tubs of spirits could be lowered until the coast was clear.

Salcott-cum-Virley, near Colchester. The turn-out for services at the church was swelled by smugglers keeping an eye on their concealed contraband. This is the village where a boatload of excise men were

seemingly found with their throats cut. They are buried in the local churchyard with the hull of their boat over the graves.

Leigh-on-Sea, celebrated for one of the few successful female smugglers, Elizabeth Little, who seems to have specialised in silk, lace and perfumes (as well as gin). An early example of girl power.

Stambridge, where the reputed Ghost Bus was in fact a horse-driven vehicle with wheels bound with thick cloth and hooves covered with heavy sponges to ensure silence when bringing goods overland from the river.

Witham – the town centre pub, The Spread Eagle, has a small window in the bar where drinkers can see into the smuggling shaft that led from roof to cellar.
At Fingringhoe (between Mersea and Colchester) there is a spreading oak tree to mark the location of a hanged smuggler (just outside the churchyard).

When Daniel London, in 1819, found a haul of 152 tubs of spirits while dredging at Old Hall Creek, Maldon, he sailed them to the custom house. The infuriated smugglers threatened to lynch him, so Daniel, in fear of his life, 'owned up' to the eleven tubs he had in fact left behind (for himself? not enough room?), and was thrown into Chelmsford Gaol.

Not just alcohol, but tea, was of great value in the eighteenth century. Two smugglers disguised as customs officers turned up at Hythe Quay in Colchester after their haul of 1,512 lbs of tea had been seized. Once at the custom house, thirty armed colleagues joined them and broke open the building to take back the bags of tea.

More recently, an attempt in 2008 to smuggle £350 million of cocaine resulted in Perry Wharrie of Loughton becoming a laughing stock. Wharrie was released on licence after serving seventeen years of a life sentence for murdering PC Frank Mason in 1988, and teamed up with international drug-runners – but their attempt to smuggle the cocaine into West Cork in Ireland became a series of amateur bungles. First, their boat capsized, then their inflatable boat was overloaded, their spare fuel tank was filled with diesel instead of petrol, and the stormy July seas resulted in the vessel sinking. The men were sentenced to a total of 85 years.

Scandals and Cover-Ups

Richard de Southchurch, the thirteenth-century Sheriff of Essex, was known as Richard the Extortioner. His reputation was earned in two different ways – first, he 'requisitioned' large stores of wheat and oats plus oxen, cattle, poultry and hams from local farms in the name of King Henry III, with plenty of this treasure trove turning up in his own home at Southchurch Hall, now in Southend-on-Sea. Then he arrested men and demanded a ransom for their release; a couple of nice little earners for which he does not seem to have been punished, though he did serve a mysterious spell in Fleet Prison in 1285.

Richard Rigby from Mistley was the Paymaster of the Forces from 1768 to 1782 and became suspiciously rich as a result. Finally, he was disgraced – but not imprisoned – and his plans for a grand house were scuppered.

The eighteenth-century Lord Sandwich was having an affair with a wannabe actress, Martha Ray, who had a fondness for the seaside. A mutual friend, Richard Rigby (again), had established fashionable tea rooms at the Naze Tower (Walton on the Naze) which became the couple's perfect hideaway. Tea was an expensive luxury at the time, with locks on tea caddies to keep the servants away! (Martha, incidentally, was shot in London by a jealous would-be-lover who had first met her at the Naze Tower.)

Someone obviously recruited the wrong man as Keeper of the House of Correction at Chelmsford between 1816 and 1822. This was when the Keeper, William Couthon, was accused, variously, of rape, negligence, frequent absences from duty, lack of co-operation, taking illegal fees, fraud and abuse! He eventually absconded and managed to avoid trial and punishment.

Was Sir William Gull, the Royal physician from Thorpe-le-Soken, in fact Jack the Ripper? Many think he was in spite of his height (6ft, which didn't tally with descriptions) and his age (seventy-one at the time of the killings).

INEFFICIENT VILLAINS

A one-handed poacher called Holden was involved in an attempted burglary in Manningtree in 1851, foiled by the local constable. One of the items left behind at the scene made it easy to trace Holden – it was his wooden hand with a glove on!

When small-time crook Donald Hume threw a headless torso out of the window of his light aeroplane when over Dengie Flats, north of Foulness Sands, he made the mistake of cutting off the legs rather than the arms. The body – found by a farm labourer on 21 October 1949 – was identified by the fingerprints as Stanley Setty, another small-time crook and colleague of Hume. The police could only prove that Hume had dumped Setty rather than murdering him, but, after serving eight years in prison in Dartmoor for complicity, he was released and later proclaimed his guilt in a lurid, sensationalised confession.

James Lee, responsible for the murder of Inspector Thomas Simmons of Romford in 1885, was arrested in London while trying to pawn the pistol used in the shooting.

Here Come the Girls

In 1615, a Lieutenant of the Tower of London, Sir Gervase Elwes, claimed that he had thwarted a plot to kill one Thomas Overbury and implicated Countess Frances Howard of Audley End, Saffron Walden. Poisoned wine, tarts and jellies were all sent into the Tower, most intercepted by Elwes. At the time, those guilty of poisoning were subjected to death by being boiled in hot water. Luckily for Frances, she confessed before her trial in 1616 and was spared because of her penitence.

Elizabeth Fry, who worked tirelessly to improve prison and social conditions in the early nineteenth century, lived in Plashet, then in Essex (now in East London). In 1810, 100,000 people were in prison, even more than at the beginning of the twenty-first century, with over two hundred crimes attracting the death penalty.

The first young lady to be brought before a court for speeding – at 67mph on her brother's motorcycle – was Mildred Petre of Coptfold Hall, Margaretting, in 1911. In her thirties, Mildred took part in several Monte Carlo rallies and also set several motorboat speed records. The 'Queen of Speed' bought a Blackburn Bluebird IV in 1930 and after forty hours of solo flight she set off around the world, this time without breaking any laws.

When Edith Thompson was executed at Holloway in 1923 for her part in the murder of her husband, her executioner went on to commit suicide, and the prison governor and chaplain retired. If Edith, from Ilford, hadn't kept the letters her lover had sent to her – and he hers – then her lifestyle would not have been dragged through the courts, and she may well have escaped such harsh retribution.

Margaret Dowse's behaviour prompted the assistant Metropolitan Police commissioner, Sir Robert Jackson, to include a question at selection boards asking candidates: 'What would you do about Margaret Dowse?' She moved around the country from one sub-post office to another, manipulating her employers until she could be trusted with the cash, then disappearing. By the time she was caught, she was wanted in forty-three different towns, and was imprisoned for five years in 1960 – eventually retiring with her partner-in-crime Stanley Turner to a boarding house in Westcliff-on-Sea.

After Susan Barber's husband was cremated at Southend-on-Sea in July 1981, she thought she had got away with poisoning him. Michael Barber's employers agreed on her receiving a £15,000 death benefit plus £3,300 per annum for each of her three children. Susan began enjoying herself hugely in her Westcliff-on-Sea home using the call-sign Nympho on her newly-purchased CB radio, apparently taking her adopted name seriously. However, delayed post-mortem results finally confirmed the presence of paraquat and Susan was sentenced to life imprisonment, with her young lover receiving a two-year sentence for conspiracy.

The former dresser of the Duke of York, Jane Andrews was probably the most famous inmate at Bullwood Hall prison in Hockley. She was imprisoned for life in 2001 when found guilty of murdering Thomas Cressman at the flat they shared in London.

THE COUNTY'S COPPERS

The first Chief Constable of Essex (1840) was Captain John Bunch Bonnemaison McHardy, a Scotsman who had never set foot in Essex before his interview for the post. He stayed in the role for forty-one years.

PC John Rough, who had lived in Orsett and Ockendon, was sent to a debtors' prison in 1842 – and lost his job as a result – because his wife had failed to pay their £35 grocery bill. (This was of course at a time when a man was liable for his wife's debts.)

Constable Thomas Kelly, a twenty-nine-year-old former paper maker, lasted just thirteen days as a police officer in 1843, losing his job after turning up 'drunk on parade'.

Stebbing PC Henry Fitch spent more than 500 hours making a model of his local church, complete with organ and floor tombs, accurately to scale – a piece of work which was so striking that it earned a place at the Great Exhibition in Crystal Palace in London.

Rules were most definitely rules in 1859. PC John Maguire ended up in the local workhouse after he was dismissed from his post in West Bergholt for buying refreshments in a public house when on duty.

Hezekiah Staines, a special constable from Bradwell, was reputedly a smuggling double agent at the end of the nineteenth century – his night and day activities being at odds with each other.

Undercover police were used as stevedores to infiltrate Tilbury Docks in 1901 to quell an illicit trade in alcohol.

When Brentwood-based superintendent Alfred Marden was disciplined and reduced in rank in 1912 for his lack of respect, bad language and unorthodox techniques, he resigned, but continued to pose as a police officer. As a result he was not only fined, but threatened with a reduced pension; a sad postscript for an officer who had earned the Merit Star during his career.

PRISON STORIES

Colchester Castle became the town gaol by 1350, but was poorly maintained and it was easy for prisoners to escape. When John Howard, the penal reformer, visited the prison in the eighteenth century, he was appalled at the conditions, but it continued to operate for two hundred years.

The first house of correction in Essex seems to be the one that opened in Corringham in 1587. This was just a year after it became a legal requirement for each county to have its own such house.

On 11 August 1746, after Culloden, 268 Jacobite prisoners were landed at Tilbury Fort. Forty-five died in the first month alone because of the inhumane conditions. A redundant gun powder magazine building in the south-east bastion was used as the prison. Other prisoners were even worse off, staying on the prison hulks with the daily threat of deadly illnesses such as typhus.

In the eighteenth century, Halstead was home to a prison with a thatched roof. It is not so surprising to find that the prison burnt down in 1781, with the loss of four lives.

The last governor of Springfield Gaol, Chelmsford (1861–81), Captain McGorrery, moved into the governor's residence within the prison's walls in 1862. Soon after, his sister and his seven-year-old son died of diphtheria, the disease having spread from the prison inmates. The remaining family moved out so that the house could be disinfected, but two weeks after moving back McGorrery's five-year-old daughter contracted scarlet fever. This time, understandably, the family moved out for good.

'The Ballad of Ilford Jail' was written in the 1860s, and ends with the enlightening insight that:

> Jonah lived inside a whale,
> He was better off there than in Ilford Jail.

The Kray twins did time at the Military Corrective Training Centre (the glasshouse) when temporarily housed in Nissen huts at Colchester Garrison, although the huts were used mainly for German POWs. Colchester Barracks is the site of the last remaining military prison in the UK, its regime much tougher than in civilian prisons.

The women in Chelmsford Prison at the beginning of the twentieth century were moved into Holloway Prison, London, when it became a women's prison. In the 1960s, Bullwood Hall at Hockley was built as a female borstal, but was redesignated as a male category C establishment in 2006.

A MACABRE SENSE OF HUMOUR

When Abraham Green, a gypsy known as Little Abel, broke into the home of Nehemiah Perry to rob him because he was unhappy about the way Nehemiah's young gypsy wife was being treated, he was confronted with a loaded shotgun and killed. Such an event would have been condoned at a time when, in preserving your own property, you could go to any lengths and not be brought to trial. The whole of

Strethall village turned out to see the corpse, which Perry subsequently hung inside the ancient church and showed it to sightseers at three pence apiece. Further than that, he packed Little Abel's corpse into a hamper and sent it off to a doctor friend in Cambridge. Although Dr Paget may have been disappointed that it was not the game he was expecting, the corpse was gifted to the Cambridge School of Anatomy – apart from the breast-bone embedded with shotgun pellets, which ended up in the museum.

Force Facts

John Harriott from Great Stambridge founded the Thames River Police in 1798 with sixty salaried men in rowing boats – armed with cutlasses – to protect the riverside merchants. It is the oldest professional body of law enforcement officers in the UK.

In 1840, the parish constables were replaced by a full-time police force in Essex. Recruits had to be literate, numerate, less than forty years of age, and over 5ft 7in tall. The first detectives were appointed in Essex in 1888.

Although the first police station in Essex was at Halstead, in the former House of Correction, the first manned police station was in Billericay, and the first purpose-built police station was opened in 1843 at Dunmow (and is still in use). The newest state-of-the-art station was built at Braintree in 1993.

Sir Evelyn Ruggles-Brise of Spains Hall, Finchingfield, introduced the borstal system of training in 1901. This was also the year that saw the introduction of fingerprint identification in Essex.

The first police cars were introduced in Essex after a successful campaign following the Honeypot Lane murders, Basildon, in an area very difficult for police to access at the time (1906). The murderers – next-door neighbours of the victims – were apprehended in spite of these disadvantages.

The first Essex police dogs were Senta (an Alsatian) and Remoh (a Doberman), purchased in 1953. Bloodhounds were trialled in 1998 for three years, with less success.

5

THE PEOPLE, FAMOUS AND NOT SO …

Unusual Names Cropping Up in Essex

The name Godsave (and similar) crops up around the Felsted area, and elsewhere, attributed to 'Roger-God-save-the-ladies' recorded in the Domesday Book. The first recorded Casanova?

A Father Christmas was buried at Dedham in the sixteenth century – although of course 'Father' was a common way of recording a man who had died without a known first name.

Zeppelina Williams was born on 24 September 1916 at Great Wigborough, just as a Zeppelin *L33* came down a mile away.

Palmer's School at Thurrock had a student listed in the 1920s as Kenny King Wong Long.

Names from local death registers include Fish Pool Neville (Ongar, 1837), Easy Pease (Billericay, 1889), Methuselah Shonk (Romford, 1902) and Valentine Card (Chelmsford, 1993).

Local birth registers list Pussie Clarke (Lexden, 1898), Win Dow (Maldon, 1886), Rosie Cheek (Grays, *c.* 1897), Dick Cock (Saffron Walden, 1852), Fanny Pricklove (Waltham Abbey, 1851), Mineral Waters (Shoebury, 1893), Ever Green (Lexden, 1847), Spinner Ball (Wanstead, 1900) and Queen Victoria Smith (Rochford, 1901).

Quirky Facts Behind Some Essex Sporting Legends

The legendary footballer, Vivian Woodward (who set a record scoring eight of the fifteen goals when England thrashed France in Paris in 1908), a long-time Clacton resident, was responsible for the design

of the main stadium in Antwerp used for the 1920 Olympic Games. Woodward was not just a footballer (after training as an architect); he played cricket and tennis (reaching the Lawn Tennis Championships twice), raced pigeons and was a dab hand at roller-skating.

Jim Peters, Dagenham-raised and a Southend-on-Sea resident, was famous for *not* winning the 1954 marathon in the Empire Games (when he collapsed just 85 yards from victory) but was also the main reason behind the provision of water stations on the route for future races over 10km.

Chelmsford schoolboy Geoff Hurst (the only player to have scored a hat-trick in a World Cup Final – in 1966 for England of course) grew up to play cricket for Essex, too, but only played one game. It was in 1962, against Lancashire, the county where he was born, and he was bowled for a duck in his second innings.

Former schoolboy chess champion and an Essex fire-fighter who forfeited his job through epilepsy is Terry Marsh from Basildon, who retired in 1987 the undefeated International Boxing Federation light-welterweight champion.

Boreham's Rod Harrington, the world's number one darts player at the end of the twentieth century, spent eighteen months as an apprentice footballer with Southend United FC and played for Essex alongside the likes of Glenn Hoddle.

Another legendary darts player, Bobby George, lives in an eighteen-bedroom house he had built in 12 acres in Ardleigh which, from the air, is shaped to look like an arrow flight.

Chigwell's Ronnie O'Sullivan, snooker champion, can play both right- and left-handed. In 1991, he was the youngest person in history to make the maximum 147, a record which still stands.

LONDON CONNECTIONS

Susan Constantin Round had a fear of dying in fire and so had a stone staircase built into her home at Danbury Place between 1826 and 1831. While staying at the Raggetts Hotel in Dover Street, London, in May 1843, the hotel caught fire, and she died while trying to retrieve a valuable bracelet.

The first female shorthand writer at the Central Criminal Court, Old Bailey, was Margaret Ball from Saffron Walden. She was in court for the last hanging sentence in Britain and was appointed Recorder of the Central Criminal Court in 1962, the first woman to hold the post.

Brooking Road and Bobby Moore Walk in East London are, of course, named after Barking-born footballers Trevor Brooking and Bobby Moore.

HOLLYWOOD CONNECTIONS

Helen Mirren, former resident of Ilford and later resident of Leigh-on-Sea, has appeared naked more often than any of her generation's mainstream actresses.

One of Liz Taylor's several husbands was Michael Wilding from Westcliff-on-Sea, a well known actor in his own right.

Jamie Lee Curtis is Baroness Haden-Guest of Saling, near Braintree, as a result of her marriage to Christopher Guest (the 5th Baron), star of *Spinal Tap*.

THE MUSICAL PEOPLE OF ESSEX

Gustav Holst wrote 'The Planets Suite' while staying at Thaxted between 1917 and 1925.

The first girl Pipe Major in the world was Edith Turnbull of the Dagenham Girl Pipers, appointed in 1937.

Ena Baga, Southend-on-Sea resident, replaced Reginald Dixon on the organ for his radio broadcasts from the Tower Ballroom at Blackpool during the Second World War – and Ena's sister, Florence, became musical director at the National Film Theatre.

Paul Simon met eighteen year-old Hornchurch secretary Kathy Chitty when she was selling tickets on the door at the Railway Inn Folk Club in Brentwood in April 1964. This was the venue for Paul's UK debut, and Kathy became his girlfriend and the inspiration for such hits as 'Kathy's Song'.

A houseboat in West Mersea called *L'Esperance* was home to the world-famous British pianist, Semprini, for many years. His BBC series ran for a record-breaking twenty-five years. After his death and cremation in 1990, his ashes were scattered in the Essex waters. He was survived by his Spanish second wife, the exotically named María de la Concepción Consuelo García Cardoso.

The New Seekers (1960s and '70s pop group) had a recording studio at Rewsalls Farm, Mersea.

Ilford's Kenny Ball – and not forgetting his jazz-men – were the first trad jazz band to play at the London Palladium Theatre.

Brian Poole and the Tremeloes, initially comprised of all-Essex lads, were the first and last band to appear on *Ready Steady Go!*

In 1964, Kathy Kirby from Ilford was the highest paid female star on British television, receiving £1,000 for each *Kathy Kirby Show*.

Dagenham's Sandie Shaw was the first British singer to win the Eurovision Song Contest – in 1967, with 'Puppet on a String'. She notched up more number ones than any other female British artist in the 1960s and became the first Brit to perform behind the Iron Curtain and the last to perform in Iran as well as the first British female to produce and own her masters and copyright.

Cockney Rebel founder Steve Harley was a reporter for the *Braintree and Witham Times* between 1969 and 1971 while living in Braintree. He also worked on the *Essex County Standard* and the *Evening Gazette*.

Suzi Quatro lived for nearly thirty years in a moated Elizabethan manor house near Chelmsford. Her first husband, Len Tuckney, was her guitarist from Romford.

Australian born Barrington Pheloung, composer (of fifty-two ballet scores for starters) and conductor, composed the theme tune for *Inspector Morse* when living in Southend-on-Sea. He was inspired by using a single rhythmic Morse code note which spells out M O R S E.

Vivian Stanshall of the Bonzo Dog Doo-Dah Band moved with his family to Southend-on-Sea after the Second World War. His parents were a tad eccentric in that his mother taught him to knit and crochet, and his father (a London accountant) roller-skated to work.

The Genesis song 'The Battle of Epping Forest' is based on an actual event when rival East End gangs fought a territorial war within its boundaries.

Billy Bragg, who moved away from Essex twenty years ago, is still known as the Bard of Barking. He still writes about the county in his lyrics.

Essex-led bands not already mentioned include Blur (Colchester), Procol Harum (Southend-on-Sea), Busted (Southend-on-Sea), Dr Feelgood (Canvey Island), The Prodigy (Braintree), Depeche Mode (Basildon), Ian Dury and the Blockheads (Upminster), Jamiroquai (Colchester) and Eddie and The Hot Rods (Southend-on- Sea).

PEOPLE YOU WOULDN'T EXPECT TO FIND IN ESSEX

Robert the Bruce, victor at Bannockburn, was allegedly born in Writtle in 1274.

A mercenary was born in 1320 in Hawkswood Manor, Sible Hedingham. This was Sir John Hawkwood, possibly the first 'soldier of fortune'. Known as the 'Diabolical Englishman', his only real talent was for terror and slaughter and he fought for and against every major power in Italy, where he died in 1394. His remains were returned to his place of birth.

The first bluestocking was undoubtedly Lady Damaris Cudworth Masham of High Laver, in the seventeenth century. She was a philosopher, the daughter of a Cambridge philosopher, with an interest in – among other things – theology and metaphysics.

A baron of the Russian Empire, one Thomas Dimsdale, was born at Theydon Garnon near Epping on 29 May 1712. Thomas became an expert on inoculation for smallpox and was invited to Russia to treat the Empress Catherine the Great and her son. They both recovered and he was rewarded with the title and with £10,000, £2,000 expenses, plus a £500 annuity, setting him up for life.

The son of an Indian chief attended Chigwell School between 1713 and 1714. It seems that 'Prince' George, son of the chief of the Yemassee Indians, and based at the time in Ilford, was funded by the Quaker Society.

Captain James Cook (yes, that one), married Elizabeth Batts at St Margaret's Church, Barking, in December 1762. He was then a warrant officer in the Royal Navy, aged thirty-four, and she was twenty-two, the daughter of a publisher who lived near Ilford Broadway. (Also, Cook's astronomer on his second voyage around the world was William Wales from Clavering.)

A Negro slave, namely Hester Woodley, died in 1767 at Little Parndon.

The Tolpuddle Martyrs (George and James Loveless and James Brine) lived at Tudor Cottages, Greensted Green, near Ongar between 1838 and 1844 on their return from transportation. Thanks to a public outcry, they had served two years of their seven-year sentence for forming a trade union to resist their (farmer) employer's wage cuts. Later, they emigrated to Ontario.

An American Bushwhacker and leading figure in the Kansas frontier fighting in the nineteenth century was Hamilton Williams, the finest horseman in south Essex. After his adventures, he retired to Tilbury, and could be seen taking long horse-rides along the Corringham and Canvey sea walls and across Benfleet marshes.

A *Titanic* survivor, Eva Hart lived in Japan Road, Chadwell Heath. She died at the age of ninety-one, on 14 February 1996.

George W. Bush's ancestors date back as far as 1391 in Messing Parish records. Reynold Bush sailed to Massachusetts in 1631 to initiate the American line. The author of *Simply Messing* (Roger Carter), points out that a Bush ancestor, fined for killing some doves, could have been castrated if he had committed the same offence a century earlier – and US history would have turned out very differently.

A recent candidate for America's First Lady was Elizabeth Kucinich, née Harper, hippie chick – complete with tongue stud – from Upminster. Elizabeth, thirty-one years younger than Dennis Kucinich, a left-wing Democratic congressman and presidential candidate, was brought up in Dennis's Cottage, Dennis's Lane, which she regarded as

an omen. At school, she was known as the Jolly Green Giant because of her height – she is a six-footer.

A Polish strongman – formerly a Cossack – lived quietly in Hockley from the mid-1950s until his death in 1962. Alexander Zass, known as Samson, could catch a woman fired from a cannon, and carry a small horse. He topped the bill at such venues as the Coliseum, Alhambra and Hippodrome.

A beauty queen who is a member of Mensa? Yes, Jade Eden, former Miss Essex, and participant in *Big Brother* 2008.

TEN PEOPLE WHO BROKE UNUSUAL RECORDS

Edward Bright (1721–50) was the 'fat man of Maldon', reputed to be the fattest man in England until his record was broken in 1809. He weighed between 44 and 47 stone at his death (accounts vary). Following a bet after his death (December 1750), seven men managed to fit into just one of his green baize waistcoats, and though some accounts quote 700 men this is in fact a reference to the seven men being men of the 'Dengie Hundred' (what is now the local council) thus seven hundred(s).

According to the *Guinness Book of Records*, the world's longest serving teacher was Colonel E.A. Loftus who moved to Essex in 1903 to teach at the Friends (Quaker) School in Saffron Walden. He went on to become the first headmaster of Barking Abbey School (founded 1922) and died in 1987 at the age of 103, when his ashes were scattered on the site of Barking Abbey.

Thorpe-le-Soken is reputed to have been the home of the much-travelled tallest man in Britain, Frederick Kempster, who (again, accounts vary) attained a height of between 7ft 8in and 8ft 4in. 'Frederick the Great', the Essex Giant, died in 1918 at the age of thirty, before the *Guinness Book of Records* was around to authenticate his claim.

Rose Harrington, the landlady at The Bell, Halstead, was apparently the oldest landlady in the country when she died aged ninety-one in 1960.

When Irene Hanson from Rayleigh gave birth to quintuplets at Queen Charlotte's Hospital in London in 1969, her five baby girls all made it against the odds. They were only the second set of all-girl quintuplets to survive, and the first live quintuplets born in Britain in the twentieth century.

The world's youngest national chess player, at four years old, was Stephanie Hale from Chigwell Row. She played in the National Mini Squad Tournament in 1999, and was the star of the Essex Junior Chess Club, all of whose members were several years older. At the age of nine, Stephanie – from a chess-playing family – became the first pupil to win a national chess scholarship to a top public school (Millfield in Somerset) and she played for England in the World Youth Chess Championships in 2005 a year later.

In September 2003, James Peters from Chelmsford set a record for the greatest number of straitjacket escapes in eight hours! He untied himself 193 times at the YMCA in Chelmsford – but whether this will come in useful later is yet to be seen.

Britain's former oldest man was made honorary skipper of a Burnham sailing club (The Narrow Seas Club) in April 2007. Henry Allingham was 110 at the time, and an early member of the club which launched in 1932. He sadly passed away in July 2009.

Fund-raiser Lloyd Scott from Rainham set a record for the slowest London Marathon in 2002 when he completed the course – in five days! He was wearing a 120lb deep-sea diving suit. Lloyd has raised over £5 million for charity since beating leukaemia himself.

Essex-based comic Lee Evans smashed his own live solo gig record in October 2007 by generating sales of 15,000 seats for his stand-up show at the O2 arena in under one hour – and the gig became the biggest ever in the history of live solo comedy.

DEFYING THE ESSEX GIRL STEREOTYPE

Prison reformer Elizabeth Fry lived in Plashet (now part of East London) in the nineteenth century after marrying merchant Joseph Fry in 1800, and spent several family holidays at Dagenham Lake.

She certainly needed a holiday with eleven children of her own, as well as her life's work with prisoners, beggars, the homeless and patients in mental asylums. Not content with that, she also set up training courses for nurses at Guy's Hospital, London, influencing the likes of Florence Nightingale. Quaker Elizabeth is the only Essex girl to feature on the back of a banknote!

One of the most vigorous campaigners for the abolition of slavery was Anne Knight from Chelmsford. She carried out door-to-door canvassing in the town and was a part of the Chelmsford Female Negro's Friends Society in the 1820s. A village in Jamaica eventually founded for freed slaves was named Knightsville in her honour.

Edith Cavell was appointed governess to the four children of the Revd Charles Powell, vicar of Steeple Bumpstead, in 1886. In 1915, when a nurse, she was to become the heroine shot by a German firing squad for helping Allied soldiers to escape.

Suffragettes from Essex played a vital role in the campaign for women's votes prior to the First World War. Sylvia Pankhurst, one of the more famous figures, lived at Woodford until her death in 1960. Among the lesser known was music-hall artiste Kitty Marion, raised in Great Dunmow and far more violent than Sylvia. Kitty spent a lot of time in prison and is said to have been the first person in Britain to have had a surveillance camera trained on her.

Pride of Essex

Andrew Battell, from Leigh-on-Sea, seems to have been the first European to travel to Central Africa and the first Englishman to describe chimpanzees and gorillas to the Western world. He died in 1620.

The Commander of the ninety-eight gun *Temeraire* at the Battle of Trafalgar (October 1805) was Sir Eliab Harvey of Rolls Park, Chigwell. Although much damaged, the *Temeraire* forced the French battleships on both sides to strike to her deadly broadsides. As one of the key ships in the action, she became known as 'The Fighting *Temeraire*' and is preserved in a famous painting by Turner. Sir Eliab – later Admiral – was an MP for Maldon and for Essex. He died in 1830 and is interred in the family crypt at Hempstead church.

Joseph Lister was born in Upton, Essex, in 1827, the son of a wine merchant. He trained as a surgeon in London and Glasgow, and is known throughout the world as the originator of antiseptics as well as other innovative ideas such as the use of tourniquets. A measure of his renown was his being offered burial in Westminster Abbey, but he chose to be buried alongside his wife (in Hampstead cemetery).

Mount Bures was the birthplace in 1830 of William Cant, son of an agricultural labourer, who emigrated aged twenty to Australia, which meant a thirteen-week sea voyage. He led a prospecting-for-gold expedition in 1854 inland, but the heat and the lack of water meant he had to return to the coast after losing a score of horses and one of his crew. He died in Australia, aged 102, leaving eight children behind him.

In 1865, Edward Whymper was the first mountaineer to conquer the Matterhorn. He lived overlooking the Thames Estuary at Southend-on-Sea from 1880 to 1906 in a four-storey boarding house which he hired in its entirety, although he only used the top rooms. Whether he just liked heights, or whether he was anti-social, has not been established.

Dr Barnardo (who opened his first charitable home 'for disadvantaged girls' in 1876 in Barkingside), had been horrified by the plight of

homeless youngsters while studying medicine in London. By the 1930s, the organisation had 188 homes caring for 8,000 youngsters. Along the way, Barnardo (a Spaniard, born and brought up in Dublin, married in East London) was in court 88 times for kidnapping, i.e. removing minors from violent or cruel parents without consent. Incidentally, he never actually qualified as a doctor.

The man whose heroic gesture of self-sacrifice failed to save his colleagues in Scott's 1912 Antarctic Expedition is remembered at his local church in Gestingthorpe. Captain Lawrence Oates was a part of that expedition which set sail from Tilbury Dock on 1 June 1910. His family home was the palatial Gestingthorpe Hall, Hedingham, a world away from the deprivation the expedition endured upon their return journey across the ice, lacking food and equipment and afflicted with frost-bite and gangrene. It was his thirty-second birthday on 17 March, when he announced that he was 'just going outside and may be some time.'

After demobilisation, T.E. Lawrence, better known as Lawrence of Arabia, bought a large part of Pole Hill at Chingford in 1919 and lived there for many years. There he finished writing his *Seven Pillars of Wisdom*, chronicling his experiences during the Arab Revolt of

1916–18. This kept the uncrowned 'King of Arabia' out of trouble while rumours about his spying activities died down.

The Essex man who lived on 2oz of food per day for five months alone in temperatures of -45°C when 9,000ft up on the Greenland ice cap, was Augustine Courtauld from Great Yeldham. The British Arctic Air Route Expedition (1930–1) set out to research the weather conditions because of the possibility of air routes over the ice caps. AC, as he was known, was happy to be left alone until a relief party could reach him, but they took months longer than envisaged because of the conditions. His home was a tent 5ft in diameter, covered in snow. Such tenacity was rewarded by George V in 1932 with the Polar Medal.

In 1990, Trevor Osben of St Osyth returned to the UK having single-handedly circumnavigated the world in his 20ft plywood sloop, *Chess*. He had taken up sailing for his health, having had asthma as a child, but the four-year trip set him quite a challenge. He'd only been sailing for two years by then, and was dismasted three times during his voyage. Trevor taught himself astro-navigation crossing the Bay of Biscay, and survived gale force winds around Gran Canaria which damaged both rudder and rigging. When he failed to find work in 1990, he set off again, this time aiming for South Africa. Sadly, he never made it, and he and his boat were never traced.

SOME ESSEX ECCENTRICS

The seventh Lord Petre of Ingatestone Hall spent six hours every day (yes, day) dressing his hair. (Eat your heart out Russell Brand). It was his theft of a lock of pretty Arabella Fermor's hair in 1712 that caused the family feud featured in Pope's *The Rape of the Lock*. Pope certainly benefited more from the incident than Petre – or Arabella – as his epic poem sold 3,000 copies in the first four days. As Peter Ackroyd put it in the *Guardian* on 2 October 2004, 'Never has so great a poem emerged from so trivial a cause.'

The monster oak tree in Hainault Forest was the venue for the annual feast organised by Daniel Day for his fellow block-makers (from East London) in the eighteenth century. He travelled to the forest in one of several fully-rigged model ships mounted on carriage frames and drawn by six horses, with out-riders and musicians. This 'private' celebration developed into a pleasure fair of such riotous proportions that the authorities stepped in and discontinued the proceedings, to the disappointment of the local crowds who had made full use of Daniel Day's hospitality, whereby he distributed goodies from the hollow trunk of the oak. A few years before he died, a large branch of the tree was blown to the ground in a storm, and his coffin was made from this. He was buried at Barking in 1767 at the age of eighty-four, but the Fairlop Fair he had established continued for over 100 years in different guises at different locations.

Sir Harvey Elwes and his nephew John may have been contemporaries of Daniel Day, but were the exact opposite in every way. The men were known as the Misers of Ashen. Sir Harvey lived in Ashen Hall, a big place which he seems to have tried to heat by means of burning one stick of wood at a time. To keep himself warm, it seems he preferred the more economic option of pacing up and down. His clothes were well-worn, his horse noticeably thin, and he and his household (he 'maintained' three servants) lived almost entirely upon game thanks to his skill at partridge setting. Not unexpectedly, Sir Harvey's favourite hobby was counting his money, but, perhaps surprisingly, after being burgled by the Thaxted gang as they were known, he would not appear against them as he regarded his time as just as valuable as his money. He died worth between £250,000 and half a million, inherited by his nephew who also inherited his frugality. John Elwes's whole system of life was founded on self-denial. He would walk miles in the rain rather than hire a conveyance; and sit hours in wet clothes rather than incur the expense of a fire. He would advance a large sum to oblige a friend, and on the same day risk his life to save paying a penny at a turnpike. He would eat meat in the last stage of putrefaction rather than allow a small profit to a butcher. Elwes, who died in 1789, was the epitome of 'penny wise and pound foolish'.

In the nineteenth century, an American millionaire by the name of Bayard Brown lived for some years at Brightlingsea and Wivenhoe. He had a rather warped sense of humour in that he heated up sovereigns in a frying pan, threw them over the side of his yacht to people in nearby boats and then watched the catchers drop the sovereigns sharply, their catch sinking into the creek. It seems he also had a habit of sitting naked aboard this same yacht.

Although he was a Wivenhoe Labour councillor after the First World War, living quietly with his wife Kate, Harry Bensley had a claim to fame just a few years earlier. Over brandy and cigars in a London club, he argued that it was possible for a man to walk around the world without being identified. As a result, he took on the largest recorded bet at the time (1907) of $100,000 pledged by John Pierrepoint Morgan, an American millionaire. He set off on 1 January 1908, complying with Morgan's conditions: he had to push a pram all the way, wear an iron mask, take just £1 and one change of underwear with him, together with some postcards he could sell, and he had to bring back a wife! Unsurprisingly, he met crowds wherever he went – presumably becoming very identifiable – and passed through twelve countries in six years, until, on the outbreak of war with just 7,000 miles to go to complete the bet, he returned to fight for his country.

In about 1860, George Fax became the 'Birdman of Essex'. He fashioned numerous pairs of wings, and used the roof of his home at Chigwell Row as a launch-pad. His spoil-sport neighbours put an end to his attempts by taking him to court as a nuisance. George's reaction was to agree that, although he was 'a good flyer' he could not 'alight very well.'

When fans of silent films went along to the Empire Cinema in Halstead in the 1930s, the piano player, Professor Taylor, sported some remarkable waistcoats. It is interesting to speculate how many of the audience knew that he made them from the skins of his pet rabbits.

Essex as a Cultural County

Ten Famous Artists
John Constable, while born over the border in Suffolk, was educated (at boarding school in Fordstreet and at Dedham Grammar) in Essex and spent many painting hours in the county, especially in the Stour Valley. One of his most famous paintings is of Hadleigh Castle.

Sir Alfred Munnings, also Suffolk-born, moved to Castle House, Dedham, in 1919 and died there on 17 July 1959. Often acclaimed as the British Degas, he was particularly renowned for his equestrian paintings.

John Nash, famous for his wartime paintings, lived in Wormingford from 1944 until his death in 1977.

Edward Bawden, born in 1903 in Braintree, became famous for his posters. After living in Great Bardfield, he moved (when a widower) to Saffron Walden, where he died in 1989. Bawden was the inspiration behind Fortnum and Mason's image in catalogues and on the shop floor.

Francis Bacon was born in Dublin and died in Madrid (1992), but spent a number of years in his house and studio at Wivenhoe. He was famous for his angry-young-man lifestyle as well as his modern works, and in 2008 his *Triptych* (1975) was sold at Sotheby's in New York for £44 million, creating a record for a contemporary work at auction.

Richard Chopping was the creator of some of the most celebrated dust-jackets in modern fiction, those of the first editions of the James Bond novels. Born in Colchester in 1917, he also lived in Wivenhoe from 1944 until his death in 2008.

Mick Cawston, born in Dagenham in 1959 (and moved to Burnham-on-Crouch in 1983), was rated the number one dog- and horse-painter in the country by 1987.

Grayson Perry, a transvestite potter from Chelmsford who has a female alter-ego called Claire, won the Turner Prize in 2003.

Michael Landy recreated the Ilford house where he was brought up as a controversial exhibit in the Tate Britain Gallery in 2004.

Mark Wallinger from Chigwell (who taught Damien Hirst when at Goldsmiths) won the 2007 Turner Prize.

Ten Famous Writers

Alfred Lord Tennyson, poet laureate, lived at Beech Hill House, High Beach from 1837 to 1840. The lines 'Ring out the old, ring in the new' were seemingly addressed to Waltham Abbey.

Ursula Bloom, long-time resident of Frinton-on-Sea before and after the 1920s, wrote 560 books (mostly romantic novels), and was in the *Guinness Book of Records* at one point as the world's most prolific writer.

Dorothy L. Sayers, creator of Lord Peter Wimsey, lived in Witham for nearly thirty years until her death in 1957.

Dodie Smith did a lot of writing for the West End stage and the American screen before returning to her beloved Finchingfield in 1953. She continued to write until her death at the age of 94. *101 Dalmatians* is inevitably recorded as her greatest success, thanks to Walt Disney, and she left £2,000 of her substantial estate (in 1990) to her last, and seventh Dalmatian, Charley.

George Granville-Barker, the poet described by T.S. Eliot as a genius, fathered fifteen children by four women, passionate in everything he did. He was born in Loughton in 1913.

John Fowles, author of such best-selling novels as *The French Lieutenant's Woman*, has a plaque on the house where he was born in Leigh-on-Sea in 1926.

Ruth Rendell lived at Shelley Grove, Loughton, as a child. In 1948 she started her writing career on the *Chigwell Times* as a junior reporter.

Her success with her Wexford novels and subsequent psychological thrillers is a global phenomenon. Her fifty novels, with many adapted for television, have made her a millionairess several times over.

Bernard '*Sharpe*' Cornwell was adopted as an infant during the Second World War by a couple in Thundersley, near Rayleigh. They were members of a strict religious sect based in Leigh-on-Sea known as the Peculiar People.

Martina Cole, born in Aveley in 1959, has won numerous prizes for her hard-hitting crime novels. Her books are stolen from Essex bookshops more so than any others!

Tony Parsons, author of the hugely successful *Man and Boy* (subsequently a film with Ian McShane) was born in Romford in 1953, and later lived in Billericay.

And some cultural curiosities

Lady Mary Wroth (born in 1587) married the owner of Loughton Hall in 1604 and began an interesting 'literary' career, writing the first prose romance by an English woman (*Urania,* published 1621) and the first sonnet sequence by a woman. The former created an outcry among members of the court and was withdrawn after six months. Mary was written of admiringly by such luminaries as Ben Jonson and was the mistress of her cousin William Herbert, 3rd Earl of Pembroke. However, by 1643, she was living in Woodford, her widowhood made uncomfortable by substantial debts.

'The Universal Mother of Mankind' was conceived in Essex because when Sir Jacob Epstein lived at Deerhurst on Baldwins Hill, Loughton, in the 1920s, a large block of marble was delivered to him from Paris, and this was shaped into his most controversial figure: 'Genesis'. Upon its completion in 1930, it was described as an 'affront to womanhood' and in the 1950s it formed part of an exhibition called Freaks of Modern Art shown by Tussaud's in Blackpool.

Colchester artist Bill Burton (1907–95) had his painting 'Eventide', a sunset of Mersea Island, on display in the flat above the corner shop in *Coronation Street*, which led to thousands of sales.

6

ESSEX AT WORK

INVENTIONS AND DISCOVERIES ROOTED IN ESSEX

The discovery of how the blood circulates around the body was down to William Harvey from Hempstead who qualified as a doctor in 1602. His findings were published in 1628.

Pioneering use of forceps in the delivery of babies can be traced back to Woodham Mortimer Hall, near Maldon. Peter Chamberlen, the resident (and surgeon), advocated the formal training of midwives and the provision of public baths. Having eighteen children of his own may well have fuelled his interest in the subject. The mass production of these forceps did not follow for another hundred years as it seems that he, and subsequent generations of Chamberlen doctors, kept the design secret.

Back in 1699, the first operational lighthouse – the Eddystone Lighthouse at Plymouth – was designed and built by Henry Winstanley, born 1644 in Saffron Walden. To raise money for his work, he founded a 'Mathematical Water Theatre' in Piccadilly, London, featuring elaborate hydraulic tableaux which were, for twenty years from 1696, a profitable and popular concern. However, Henry and his lighthouse were wiped out together in a great storm in 1703.

Experiments to establish the speed of sound were made from the tower of St Laurence Church, Upminster. The man responsible was William Derham (1689–1716).

The patented grinding engine invented by Aaron Hill prior to 1714 was used to grind beech nuts from Epping Forest for his Beech Oil Company. Squabbles with shareholders, however, meant that the company was dissolved after just two years.

An 'unsolvable' problem, according to Sir Isaac Newton, was in fact solved in 1733 in Sutton, Essex, by Chester Moor Hall, born in Leigh-on-Sea. He discovered a lens system which meant that a telescope free of colour distortion could be constructed, but, in attempting to keep

his work a secret by commissioning different lens makers to work on the concave and convex halves, he had not reckoned that they would sub-contract the work – to the same person, George Bass, an acquaintance of John Dolland (*sic*). Everyone has heard of Dollond and Aitchison, but who has heard of Chester Moor Hall?

The first unsinkable lifeboat was invented in 1784 by Lionel Lukin who experimented on Doctor's Pond in Great Dunmow – a long way from the coast. His design was improved upon by another Essex man, George Palmer of Nazeing Park, Waltham Abbey.

The Darby Steam-Digger, built at Lodge Farm, Pleshey, near Chelmsford, won a prize in about 1879, but the digger was not taken up by farmers who were more used to horses. Its inventor, farmer Thomas Darby, must have been sorely disappointed at its resultant lack of commercial success.

R.E. Crompton and Company, Chelmsford, employed 600 men at its peak at the end of the nineteenth century. Its founder, Colonel Rookes Evelyn Bell Crompton, died in 1940 at the age of 96 after the company had developed, among other things, the use of electric lighting installed at Buckingham Palace and Windsor Castle, and the first electric trains which ran on Southend Pier.

Argon, after its discovery at the beginning of the twentieth century, became the gas of choice for high-temperature process or metal working. The discovery was the work of physicist John Rayleigh (later Lord), confusingly born in the Maldon area – rather than Rayleigh –

in 1842. His work merited the Nobel Prize for Physics in 1904, the first time it had been presented to an Englishman.

Britain's first official radio broadcasts were made from Marconi's New Street Works in Chelmsford in 1920 by Dame Nellie Melba, the Australian singer. Marconi was the first radio factory in the world when it started life in 1899 at Hall Street, Chelmsford, on the site of a former silk factory, its first experimental broadcasts being made from an army hut in Writtle.

In the mid- and late 1920s, Plesseys of Ilford was the site for John Logie Baird, then living in Ilford, to perfect his invention: television. As a result, the world's first working television (1929) was christened the Plessey Baird.

In 1947, the catamaran was invented by the Prout family of boat-builders on Canvey Island. A smaller version won the first cross-channel dinghy race in 1956, and two of the Prout boys were national kayak-racing champions. The company's export success resulted in the Queen's Award for Industry in 1989.

SIX INNOVATIVE ESSEX BUSINESSES

Early in the nineteenth century, the first sugar factory in Britain started up at Ulting. It was based by the river because barges were so important in moving supplies, but could not survive commercially once the price of cane sugar dropped.

Alfred Harman, founder of the photographic company Ilford, started business in the basement of his house in Cranbrook Road, Ilford, and went public in 1898 with capital of £380,000. The name of this part of Essex is now known internationally.

At the beginning of the twentieth century, the Mersea Shell Crushing Company crushed limpets, an imported pest found on oysters, to make chicken grit.

The Ford factory in Dagenham cost £5 million pounds to build in the late 1920s and was known as the Detroit of Europe, covering as much as 300 acres; 22,000 piles had to be sunk into the unstable marshland to support the weight of the factory. Ford produced 360,000 military vehicles and more than 250,000 V8 engines during the Second World War when its work-force trebled. When the factory expanded even further after the war, Ford became one of the first businesses in Britain to use computers. Now, it is one of the greenest factories in Europe, focusing on such components as gearboxes rather than cars; the site is powered by three giant wind turbines.

The total automation of cigarette-making started in Basildon in 1960. HRH The Duke of Edinburgh threw the switch at the Carreras cigarette factory, starting the first operation of its kind in the world.

Peng Travel in Romford started in 1971 as the only tour operator in Britain to specialise in naturist holidays. Its German owner sold the business when it had grown to control 90 per cent of the UK's naturist travel market.

SOME EMBARASSING ESSEX ENTERPRISES

Daniel Defoe may have been a very successful author, but lost several thousand pounds after putting all his money into a pantile factory at

Tilbury in the seventeenth century. He employed 100 families, making an initial profit of £600 per annum from the sale of bricks and tiles, but by 1703 (when he was imprisoned for his religious views) the business was already struggling.

Fosbery of Barking, makers of marine life-saving appliances, distress signals and lifebuoys, made the life jackets for the *Titanic*. The blame for the shortfall can no doubt be placed on other shoulders because Fosbery stayed in business for another seventy years and more.

TEN LOST ESSEX MONEY SPINNERS

Infected oak tissue and sulphate nodules found on the beaches do not sound like much, but they were the basis of a thriving seventeenth-century industry, especially around Walton on the Naze and Frinton-on-Sea. Galls and copperas (the 'proper' terminology) were gathered from the trees and cliff bases where they occurred naturally, and mixed on the foreshore in hazardous conditions to produce black dye. The biggest export market was Portugal, whose women used black cloth more than any other, and the Walton copperas house flourished for many decades until the Essex tanning and cloth industries went into decline. For over a century, nothing grew on the grounds polluted by these processes.

Gosfield in North Essex was the centre of a thriving population of straw-plaiters from 1790, earning £1,700 in one year for the village women and children working from home. The idea was advanced by the first Marquis of Buckingham at Gosfield to provide income for the rural poor, and he was one of the keenest promoters of the straw hat, setting a fashion copied by his congregation and further afield. There were plenty of raw materials in the vicinity to make straw bonnets and hats and, by 1871, nearly 4,000 people were employed as straw-plaiters in a cottage industry spread around Castle Hedingham, Braintree and Halstead. By 1900 however, straw-plaiters had all but disappeared, such are the vagaries of fashion and cheap imports.

When Edward Ind bought a small brewery beside the River Rom in 1799, he could not have envisaged that the name Ind Coope (the Coope brothers joined him in 1845) would become such a big name in Essex and far beyond. The brewing industry grew in the area to such an extent that Salvation Army missionaries, arriving in 1881, referred to Romford as a 'brewery blighted town.' The business survived in the town until 1997.

When the wool trade died out in Essex in the early nineteenth century owing to Northern mechanisation, the silk weaving trade took off and Braintree dominated its production thanks to two families, the Warners and the Courtaulds. The Courtauld family date back to the Huguenots, and laid the foundations of their empire in a weatherboard workshop in Braintree with power supplied by a donkey. George Courtauld opened a silk mill in the area in 1809, and the company became world-famous for their crêpe, a hard, stiff silk used for mourning clothing, so essential for the Victorians. By 1850, over 2,000 people were employed in Courtauld's three silk mills, and by 1894 the factory was running 100 looms by water power. In 1895, Warner and Son moved to Braintree specialising in high quality fabrics. They wove the velvets for the coronation gown of King Edward VII, and supplied ceremonial clothing for King George VI, Queen Elizabeth II and the Prince of Wales. Weaving ceased in 1971 but the last handloom silk weavers in England remain at the Working Silk Museum in Braintree, making fabrics for stately homes and palaces all over the world.

In 1812, a French émigré and his daughters settled in Coggeshall and taught the local women how to decorate net – known universally as Coggeshall lace. At its peak, Coggeshall supplied lace to Liberty in London, and it has been made into dresses for Queen Mary, Queen Elizabeth II, Princess Margaret and Princess Alexandra. Only a few traditional, isolated lace makers now remain in the area.

From the Victorians onwards, the medicinal properties of local mineral waters gave rise to several successful spas – at Witham, Hockley and Dovercourt – and other wells that flourished for varying periods including those at Havering, Vange, Woodford, Chigwell, Upminster, South Weald, Felsted and Mistley. There were many tales of miraculous cures including 'Farmer Cash's Famous Medicinal Vange Water'. This was sold at the equivalent of £20 a pint until sanitary authorities in the 1920s found it unfit for either drinking or domestic use!

Brick-making was a thriving industry in Essex until the twentieth century. Seven million bricks per annum were manufactured at Vange alone using earth from marshland mixed with ash, chalk and sand, the materials brought to the works on 90-ton barges. Grays was another thriving source, plus Stock, Hadleigh and Great Wakering.

The Royal Gun Powder Mills at Waltham Abbey were established in the seventeenth century, the gunpowder being transported by barge, and its production reliant on water power. It is said that the gunpowder used by Guy Fawkes, and the explosives used in the Dam Busters raids, were manufactured here. The Crimean War of 1853 to 1856 meant that large amounts of gunpowder were needed, and the site expanded. By the end of the nineteenth century, gunpowder was being replaced by chemical explosives, and new buildings were constructed to produce materials such as cordite. The industry stopped finally after the Second World War, the mills becoming an explosives research establishment which closed in the 1990s. Essex seems to have been the centre of gunpowder production, as Kynoch & Co. opened up in 1896 at Fobbing with the same idea. This explosives factory employed 600 and created a mini-town – called Kynochtown – with houses for workers plus a school, post office and even a women's football team. It had a short life, closing in 1919.

Aviation Traders at Southend Airport blazed the trail for package holidays, flying charters to Ostend from 1949, thanks mainly to the pioneering Freddie Laker. Early disputes involved deciding who had priority on the runways – pilots or local harvesters. By 1966, Laker Airways was instrumental in initiating low-cost fares, including New York with Skytrain (from 1977). Skytrain went bust in 1982 once established airlines put pressure on its prices, around the same time that the television series *Airline*, starring Roy Marsden, arrived on screen, inspired by Laker's exploits.

Yardley, still an international name for cosmetics and perfume (especially English Lavender), relocated to Basildon in 1966 after nearly two hundred years in business. Although the modern design of the building earned a Royal Institute of British Architecture Award, the business itself went into receivership in 1998. The brand name was sold to Wella, and the site sold off.

Six Famous Businesses in Essex

Crittall (windows) have been operating out of Braintree since 1864. Frank Crittall was the first employer in the world to introduce a five-day week back in 1930. Prototype houses built for staff were the first example in England of a 'Modern Movement' style just after the First World War, and the resultant Silver End Village (near Witham) is now a designated conservation area. Crittall supplied the elaborate bronze doors, each weighing one-and-a-half tons, for the members' entrance to London's County Hall in 1924.

Bata (shoes) sent over four million pairs of shoes overseas soon after their launch in 1932 on the East Tilbury marshes. Thomas Bata, the Czech entrepreneur, sent some employees to Czechoslovakia for training and was another employer who built an estate for his employees with, apart from housing, a ballroom, cinema and even a daily newspaper. Bata shoes are now mainly manufactured overseas, but they still have a presence at Tilbury.

Tiptree (jams) was founded in 1885 by A.C. Wilkin and was originally called The Britannia Fruit Preserve Company. In the early twentieth century, it had its own railway line called the Crab and Winkle Line, to make the transport of jam to London easier, but too much jam was being stolen to make it viable. The factory has its own museum and shop, and the preserves are prepared using mainly Essex-grown fruit.

Clinton Cards is based in Loughton and is the largest specialist retailer of greetings cards in the United Kingdom with seven hundred shops (2008). The first shop was opened by Don Lewin in 1968 in Epping, who had started by selling cards from the back of his car in East London. Clinton is his son's name.

Britvic (British Vitamins Products Company) was founded in Chelmsford in the nineteenth century, and continues to thrive.

Amstrad, in Brentwood, famously founded by Alan Sugar in 1968, was acquired by Sky in a £125 million deal in 2007.

ESSEX ENTERPRISE IN ACTION

Sheep-rearing was one of the tasks undertaken by the monks in Coggeshall Abbey, founded in 1140. As a result, they are credited with starting the wool trade which brought prosperity to Essex. The monks were also said to have been early producers of bricks, another industry developed throughout Essex.

Romford Market (founded in 1247) acquired a reputation for the provision of leather goods by the sixteenth century (a local industry), and the expression 'go to Romford to be new-bottomed' was a reference to the leather breeches on sale.

John Mills, a tea dealer, opened the Colchester and Essex Bank in Colchester High Street in 1787 in partnership with the Twining Brothers.

Joseph Stannah's Ironworks started out in Boreham in 1911 to produce lifts, and was known locally as the Nuts and Bolts Works. His name lives on in the Stannah Stairlift.

In 1941, the Sterling Refrigerator Company in Dagenham took on a contract to produce 50,000 machine guns although they had no experience in making weapons.

Jonathan Ive from Chingford became the senior vice-president of Apple in California having produced the iPhone and the iMac. Customers in 2007 included George W. Bush and our own queen.

7

FISHING AND FARMING, FOOD AND FLUIDS

FLOUNDER, FLAT FISH AND THE REST

Oyster beds were flourishing in areas such as Southend-on-Sea in the eighteenth century, and were so prosperous that, in 1724, 500 fishermen from Kent pillaged the beds, treating them as common property, until the intervention of local constables. But this is not the earliest evidence of oyster fishing – piles of oyster shells excavated around Foulness, Heybridge and Brightlingsea date from Roman times. By the nineteenth century, some 144 million oysters a year were being sold in the streets of London alone – apart from those being exported – and, as a result, the Colne Fishery Company employed 500 smacks and 2,000 men in the industry. Oyster beds at other Essex locations such as Burnham and Mersea were similarly prolific, with smaller fisheries such as Brightlingsea bringing in 49,000 oysters in a six-week round trip in 1887. In its heyday, Essex supplied 70 per cent of the world's consumption of oysters. Colchester still celebrates the beginning of the season in October with a shellfish feast – with the addition of traditional gin and gingerbread. It seems that Colchester oysters are being assessed for regional status alongside Parma ham and Parmesan cheese; quite an achievement, and a long time coming. These days, the industry is based on West Mersea.

The importance of sprats to the population of Essex is shown in their being known as 'weavers' beef' especially around the Colchester area, once home to many of the Essex weavers. There used to be a Sprat Day in Colchester, taking place in November. Conversely, just a few miles away, thousands of tons of Brightlingsea sprats were used as manure by local farmers in the nineteenth century.

Barking was associated with fishing from the Middle Ages onwards (when it was compulsory to eat fish on Fridays). At one time, it seems to have had the greatest fishing fleet in the world with seventy ships of over 40 tons tying up there in 1814, and 225 fishing smacks in 1850. Victorian Samuel Hewett was an important figure in the area because he came up with the idea of using ice to preserve the fish, meaning the fishing fleet could be kept at sea for as long as eight weeks at a time. By 1862 local fishermen – including Hewett – relocated to Grimsby when their fishing docks opened with easier access to the North Sea.

Until 1220, fishing rights were a royal prerogative in Leigh-on-Sea. Luckily this did not continue as little else was available for winter food. Leigh-on-Sea, with the biggest cockle output in Britain, continues to sell fish (including cockles) along its sea-shore.

Whitebait was particularly plentiful in the eighteenth century in the Thames Estuary, where the first recorded Whitebait Feast took place at Dagenham in 1766. Elizabeth Young and her family founded a whitebait business on the Thames in 1805 and moved to Leigh-on-Sea some years later because their fishing activities were suffering as the quality of the Thames water deteriorated. They became famous for their shrimps, and in 1946 produced the first commercial frozen products after they too had moved to Grimsby.

The proximity of the North Sea for fishing as well as the estuaries meant that a huge variety of fish was once available around the Essex coastline. Apart from the oysters, cockles, sprats and whitebait, local catches pre-pollution included flounder, dab, plaice, sole, eels, halibut, turbot, brill, lobster, cod, haddock, whiting, herring, trout, pike, perch, chub, gudgeon, roach, tench and salmon.

To go with all this fish, it had to be an Essex chippie that set up the world record for dishing up a portion of chips in February 2007!

To peel and slice the potatoes, then fry and wrap the chips, Henley's in Wivenhoe recorded just 221 seconds in the *Guinness Book of Records*.

More Food with a Face

'Local' birds such as rook, woodpecker, jay, plover, moorhen, sparrow, curlew and wigeon were once regularly eaten in Essex. Nineteenth-century game included partridges, geese, puffin and hawks.

In medieval Essex, Hainault Forest was home for over five hundred pigs, with two boys employed to knock down acorns from the oak trees to supply fodder. There was a piggery in Billet Lane (Romford) as recently as 1948, and names such as Hog Hill Road and Hog's Lane remain as reminders. After the Second World War this traditional 'Essex pig' found less favour than faster-growing, commercial breeds when quantity overtook quality. The Essex pig is officially classified as extinct (the breed having amalgamated with others by the 1960s) but, thanks to one farmer – John Crowshaw – who did not amalgamate his herd, it is on the verge of being reintroduced to the world. Perhaps Essex Ham Cake, a traditional bacon product, will also be seen again.

The greatest sheep owner in Essex in the eleventh century was Baron Swein of Rayleigh Castle, with 4,000 grazing animals. Tilty sheep, tended by monks in the local abbey two hundred years later, produced vast amounts of fine wool which was exported throughout Europe.

Later still, it seems that many sheep farmers in Australia and New Zealand owed their success to Thomas Sturgeon, breeder of fine quality merinos 'in Essex', who supplied all the rams they asked for.

From the sixteenth to the eighteenth centuries, rabbits were bred for consumption in a specially built and spacious warren at Little Ilford.

The county was famous for rearing beef cattle, resulting in an Essex inhabitant at one time being known as an Essex Calf. This seems to have been an insult based on one Essex lad who reputedly – to free a calf whose head was jammed in the bars of a gate – chopped off the calf's head! In turn, the county's calves, famous for their larger-than-average size, were known as 'Essex lions'.

The Essex dairy cow seems, sadly, to have joined the dodo. The largest single supplier of milk to the London market at the turn of the twentieth century was Lord Rayleigh Dairies which went into receivership in 1996. As a result, the dairy farms that supplied them are now near extinct.

Chelmsford Chronicle 3 August 1787:

> *Wanted: A Dairy Maid to Milk Eight Cows, Morning and Evening; she must understand making of good bread and baking, take care of the poultry, and pick them for the table, clean two garrets, bed chambers, and help at the wash, and assist in the kitchen if wanted. Enquire at the White Heart,* (sic) *Chadwell-Heath for Henry Birds, Esq., Vallence, Dagenham, Essex. She must be a single Woman.*

Those were the days.

Essex Specialities

The breasts of two dozen birds (four and twenty blackbirds) with added fat for flavour were used as a filling for a suet pie by Essex marsh men more than a hundred years ago. Rook Shooting Day was held on 12 May across Essex, although the strong taste of rook was masked with onion and bacon. Even during the Second World War, Rook Pie was still popular, especially among the poor.

Ewes' cheese (dating back to Domesday) was popular in the Elizabethan period, produced mainly in the East of Essex – Canvey

Island was still producing it in the seventeenth century. Other parts of Essex produced Essex cheese from cows' milk, but this was less moist than ewes' cheese and didn't 'keep' as long. In the sixteenth century, Essex was producing cheeses 'wondered at for their massiveness.'

Honey, honey, honey. Another Domesday book entry recorded 615 hives in 130 apiaries in Essex – the highest in the country. By the beginning of the nineteenth century, England was the lead bee-keeping country, with honey from Braintree and Bocking acclaimed as producing its finest examples. Local nineteenth-century witticism: When did a lion yield honey in Essex? When bees stored their honey in the walls of the Lion Hotel, Ongar.

More sweetness in Essex came from candied eringo (or eryngo), with a taste similar to liquorice. It may not be a household name these days, but, thanks to its aphrodisiac qualities, it was a medieval version of Viagra. The sea holly, from the roots of which the sweetmeat is made, grows wild along the coast in Essex and was preserved with sugar and orange-flower water. Falstaff refers to it in Shakespeare's *The Merry Wives of Windsor*: 'let it … snow eringoes'. The peak of production was in the seventeenth and eighteenth centuries, when packets of candied eringo (at four shillings and more per pound) were presented to distinguished visitors – including the Bishop of London and Queen Charlotte – by Colchester Corporation.

Essex breads at one time included dannick (from the North of the county, perhaps a Danish name) made from stoneground wheatmeal and served hot with butter, paddles (from Chelmsford areas) in the shape of a small spade or paddle, and the Essex huffer, a round loaf cut into triangles and eaten like a teacake. A modern version of the huffer, or huffa, can still be found in traditional, rural Essex pubs, its name deriving from huff or puff to describe its lightness.

At the beginning of the twentieth century, Essex Pudding was being dished up in local homes; a boiled batter pudding served with gravy, served as a first course before poultry or roast beef.

A popular Epping speciality was pork sausages made with beef suet, a distinctive flavour similar to venison, and perhaps even including venison in the 'secret' recipe. Epping butter was also famous, with merchants trading in what is now Buttercross Lane (the cross was pulled down in 1781).

Other Essex specialities which are actually produced in the county include the Little Scarlet strawberry (exclusive to the Wilkin jam family in Tiptree) and the Early Rainham cabbage (advertised since 1876 but less evident since the 1950s).

ESSEX FOODIES

Thomas Wood, a Billericay miller born in 1719, needed to diet after ballooning to over 20 stone in his forties, which affected both his health and his temperament. For two years, he lived on a pudding made from one pound of crushed sea biscuits, two eggs and 3 pints of skimmed milk, the whole being boiled and divided into portions which he ate at set times as an aid to his digestion: 1 a.m., 4 a.m. and 12 noon. He then devised an even tougher regime with a new 'pudding' made from 1½ pints of skimmed milk and 1lb of coarse flour, and lived on this for fifteen years. His diet attracted plenty of interest, but he was the only one who had the will power to stick to it; not too surprising, perhaps.

Until the late 1860s, sheep drovers and cattlemen who stopped off on the Hockley/Rayleigh border for refreshment favoured The Drovers public house, not just for their beer and food. These macho types, often Welsh, with their dusty working clothes and work-hardened hands, had a particular yearning for jam puffs before continuing their journey to London. The men often stayed in Essex for a fattening up period for their livestock (which could also include thousands of geese) to ensure they did not arrive too lean after such a long journey.

Dagenham was nicknamed 'corned beef city' in the 1950s because they ate so much of it. During rationing, when fresh meat was in short supply, corned beef from New Zealand was the area's favoured substitute.

Manningtree was renowned for its roasted (whole) ox, cooked with 'a pudding in his belly' according to Shakespeare's *Henry IV*. The same play also refers to the amount of drinking that went on at Manningtree at Whitsun so the roast ox (and the drinking) were no doubt part of an annual medieval fair.

Essex Farming

Because saffron was in demand for its medicinal qualities between 1347 and 1350 when the Black Death was ravaging the country, the saffron crocus was cultivated throughout England. Later, saffron was in demand as a dye for wool, until the collapse of the wool trade in the eighteenth century. The Essex soil was particularly favourable for the crop, and this is how the town of Saffron Walden got its name, with the crop harvesters being known as Crokers. There has been a steady decline in the use of saffron, and hence its cultivation, since the seventeenth century, but the saffron cake continues – now associated with Cornwall. It takes as much as 150,000 flowers to produce one kilogram of dried saffron, making it the most expensive spice in the world, retailing in the twenty-first century at £3,750 per lb. (Note that Saffron Walden was also famous for its hollyhocks at the beginning of the twentieth century, the flower killed off by a mysterious infection.)

In 1594, John Norden – a cartographer and writer – produced an Essex map and description which referred to Essex as the English Goshen, 'the fattest of the lande' comparable to an area of biblical Palestine flowing with 'milke and hunneye.'

Historically, most Essex folk worked in agriculture or rural crafts until the agricultural depression. (Note that 10,000 people in Essex still work on farms.) However, large numbers of Scottish farmers came here at the end of the nineteenth century to take advantage of low land prices. They brought their own cattle, hiring an entire train if necessary, and changed the agricultural output from corn-fields (one of which is now the ground of FC Brightlingsea Regent!) to grass and turnips, also developing a new strain of malting grain, which to some extent took over from barley.

In 1890, General William Booth started up the Salvation Army Colony at Hadleigh to provide opportunities for deprived and impoverished people from the East End, all of whom had to be bathed and fumigated on arrival. The farm comprised 3,200 acres with additional plans for a brickworks, pottery, wharf and workshops. By 1898, all his ambitions were achieved, and there were 1,300 fruit trees, an 80-acre market garden producing salad crops, flowers, soft fruits and 'Colony' honey from the beehives, together with a dairy farm, granary, piggeries, mill, a 10-acre rabbit warren and a 26-acre poultry farm. There is still a weekly farmers' market today on what remains of the original colony.

Essex Quakers pioneered the production of sugar from sugar beet, setting up the country's first sugar beet plant at Ulting, near Chelmsford, in 1832. They were interested in supplanting slave-grown sugar, so contrary to the Quakers' beliefs. Lack of capital meant it only lasted two years, but another factory was established a century later (1925) at Felsted, part of the British Sugar Corporation, processing over 350 tons of white sugar in one day.

Crops produced on a large scale in Essex include the Beauty of Essex potato, Essex Red Clover, beans, peas, rhubarb, asparagus, pickling onions, cauliflowers and mustard seed. Two main varieties of Essex apple are the Discovery, and the D'Arcy Spice (the latter originating from 1785 in Tolleshunt D'Arcy).

Tobacco was grown at Tilty, near Dunmow, during the Second World War – a time when it was scarce. Their enterprising vicar advertised in the parish magazine that he would pass on the secret of how to 'cure' the crop to anyone paying five shillings towards the cost of restoring the church tower. A national newspaper picked up on his enterprise, and he received hundreds of payments from smokers – and wannabe traders – outside the county, enabling him to preserve the tower.

TEN HERBS GROWN IN ESSEX

Rosemary
Coriander
Thyme
Parsley
Sorrel
Horseradish
Sage
Dill
Marjoram
Fennel

ESSEX IN A GLASS

Cider production can be traced back to the seventeenth century in Fyfield, to the eighteenth in Colchester, and the nineteenth in Ramsden Bellhouse, and Essex whisky was made in Colchester in the early nineteenth century.

Hops were grown in Castle Hedingham for three centuries, until about 1887, with over 200 acres at one time. Sible Hedingham was the last place in the county for hops to be grown on this scale, and they were considered by some to be the best in Essex. Hops can still be found growing wild in some hedgerows around the Hedinghams, particularly along the river banks.

The first maltsters in Great Dunmow were reputedly the monks at Tilty Abbey. The maltings produced malt until the late 1940s, and was then restored fifty years later – it still produces 27 tonnes of malt every year for the production of beer and lager.

Ind Coope (now part of Allied Breweries) began life in 1799 as a small brewery attached to The Star Inn in Romford High Street. By the 1850s, there were nearly one hundred breweries in Essex. Additionally, the Epping Brewery Company was held in such esteem that it sent regular supplies of quality beer and ales to the Old Bailey in London. Much later (in 2005) Ridley's at Hartford End, built in 1842, sold the brewery to Greene King, its bigger East Anglian rival. Comparative newcomers are the Crouch Vale Brewery at South Woodham Ferrers, established in 1981 by two CAMRA enthusiasts, a welder and a civil servant. One of their successes has been Essex Boys Bitter.

Because a) the Essex climate of low rainfall and plenty of sunshine is conducive to wine-making and b) the flinty soil structure – especially in North Essex – is similar to that of the famous wine-growing regions of France, a number of vineyards thrive in the county. The oldest commercial vineyard in East Anglia and the first one to have its own, prize winning, Real Ale Brewery (The Felstar) is at Felsted. Having said that, legend has it that the Romans grew grapes on Mersea Island, and there is still a vineyard there, whose specialities include Mersea

Mehalah and Mersea Native, plus, from their own brewery, Mersea Mud, and Oyster, which has local oysters added. Fobbing, Great Bardfield, Hedingham, Debden, Great Waltham, Boxted, Ongar, Purleigh, Great Sampford, Stock – all these villages, and more, have produced fine wines. Varieties include the Essex Bacchus (scented and dry), Reichsteiner ('honeyed' dry or medium), Huxelrebe (dry white) and, more recently, Pinot Noir.

Did You Know?

. . . that The Railway Tavern, Brightlingsea, brewed its own ale, named the Crab and Winkle, giving it the same name as the railway line that used to run through the town?

. . . that Frederick Charrington, a member of the brewery dynasty (1850–1936), spent his life campaigning against the ill effects of alcohol? As part of this grand plan, he opened a home for alcoholics on Osea Island, because it was one of the rare places that alcohol was not obtainable. He forgot to reckon with enterprising Essex folk who saw a way of selling alcohol to a desperate market – straight from their boats!

. . . that the Great Vine at Hampton Court Palace, the oldest and largest known vine in the world, is believed to have started life as a small cutting from the now defunct Black Hamburgh vine at Valentine's Park in Ilford?

. . . an early fan of oysters (from Paglesham) was Benjamin Disraeli, who wrote of them enthusiastically while staying in Southend-on-Sea in 1833?

. . . that The Bell Inn, at Horndon-on-the-Hill, has pinned a hot cross bun to the ceiling beams every Good Friday since 1901 when a new landlord took over? This stems from a more general custom in Essex kitchens when, until the Second World War when such luxuries were just not available, hanging up a dried bun was believed to ward off bad luck: anyone ill the following year would have a small piece of bun broken off and crumbled into a glass of milk and water (although there is no record of 'cures').

. . . that barley was introduced to the area by Thomas Tusser, the Rivenhall-born farmer who wrote *Five Hundredth Points of Good Husbandry* in 1580?

8

ESSEX AT PLAY

Oh I Do Like to be Beside the Seaside

Southend-on-Sea has the longest pier in the world, at 1.33 miles. It was begun in 1889 and extended in 1898 to accommodate steamers bringing day-trippers from London.

When the tide is out, there is over a mile of mudflats.

Southend also offers the biggest annual free air-show in Europe.

Its Kursaal was the world's first-ever theme park, pre-dating America's Coney Island. The Kursaal opened as a marine park in 1901, but the grounds were closed in 1973. Its long-time proprietor, (C.J. Morehouse), was a 'real-life' cowboy in the Wild West. During the First World War the main attraction in the grounds was a replica of the British trenches at Ypres (it stayed open throughout the war). The launch of the Wall of Death in 1929 was the first such act featured in Europe – dare-devil motorcyclists performing jaw-dropping feats along the vertical face of a 20ft circular wooden wall.

The resort has the biggest amusement park in Essex – Adventure Island, with its latest roller coaster, Rage, the biggest to be built in England, in 2007.

Southend's greyhound stadium, dating from 1933, was also used by Southend United Football Club until their own ground was built. The last race was on Boxing Day 1985 (it is now a retail park).

Clacton-on-Sea lays claim to the largest, rather than the longest, pier in the world, and the town's cinema – Flicks – has been described as the largest cinema screen in Essex.

READ ABOUT ESSEX . . .

The earliest written reference to Essex is probably that by the Roman historian Tacitus who mentions Colchester (or, rather, Camulodunum) in *The Annals of Imperial Rome* within the chapter 'Nero and his Helpers' describing a settlement there. This of course was the settlement burned down in Boudicca's Iceni rebellion.

Jane Austen makes several references in *Emma* to Southend-on-Sea at the time it was establishing itself as a spa town (publication was 1816). Emma prohibits talk of Southend-on-Sea as she has never even seen the sea and is envious of Mrs Knightley who has spent the autumn there. It appears that Mrs Knightley 'never found the least inconvenience from the mud' – unlike some more recent visitors, perhaps.

Barnaby Rudge and *Great Expectations* reveal Charles Dickens' familiarity with the county. The first begins with a description of Epping Forest in 1775 and also features Chigwell and its public house, The King's Head, believed to be the model for The Maypole. Dickens once hired a steamer from London to Southend, and it is, almost certainly, this journey that gave him the detail and insight he needed when describing the mud flats and river at the end of *Great Expectations*. The Lobster Smack on Canvey Island is reputed to be the dirty pub featured in this latter novel, the hostelry where Pip spent the night. Indeed, the infamous Magwitch says of himself that 'I first became aware of myself down in Essex, thieving turnips.'

Like Dickens, other Victorian writers sometimes disguised the Essex locations – Mary Braddon, for instance, queen of the melodrama, disguised Ingatestone Hall as Audley Court in *Lady Audley's Secret*. H.G. Wells, however, had no such reservations. When the Martians invaded in *War of the Worlds*, they:

passed through Tillingham, which, strangely enough, seemed to be quite silent and deserted, save for a few furtive plunderers hunting for food. Near Tillingham they suddenly came in sight of the sea, and the most amazing crowd of shipping of all sorts that it is possible to imagine.

Soon after, 'a Martian appeared, small and faint in the remote distance, advancing along the muddy coast from the direction of Foulness.' Many other Essex villages are mentioned, including Maldon, the town from where the protagonists escaped across the Channel.

A more chilling Essex location is that of Purfleet, featuring prominently as the location of a large lunatic asylum in *Dracula*. The superintendent of this institution, Dr John Seward, is described as Van Helsing's 'old and true friend.' Count Dracula himself is the owner of a house called Carfax, near the asylum.

Walton backwaters, part of the Essex marshes, were the setting for Arthur Ransome's 1930 book *Secret Water* which is one of the *Swallows and Amazons* series. *The Snow Goose*, written by Paul Gallico in 1941, is set on the Essex marshes during the First World War and George Orwell's *Nineteen Eighty Four* gives Colchester the dubious accolade of being the target for a nuclear attack.

'Miles away, in the mist and rain of the Essex marshes, a satanic priest has created a hideous creature' is part of the introduction to Dennis Wheatley's 1953 novel *To The Devil a Daughter*. Kathleen (or K.M.) Peyton is said to have been inspired by a farm near Stow Maries which gave her the name *Flambards* for a popular 1960s series of novels – she also features a defunct airfield nearby.

The popular *Lovejoy* books of the '60s by Jonathan Gash include many references to villages such as West Mersea and Belchamp Walter. Ruth Rendell appears to have had a soft spot for Epping Forest, setting some of her fiction there, and in fact the hilly area of Loughton close to the forest is now called Little Cornwall from her description in her 1974 novel, *The Face of Trespass*.

. . . AND READER RECORDS

Barking was the first authority in Essex to provide a public library service, and Alexander Glenny was the first recorded borrower on 1 June 1889. Not only that, but there are more reading groups in Essex than any other English county.

RETAIL THERAPY

The first town in the country to have a Tesco supermarket was Maldon – in a converted cinema. The first pedestrian precinct in Britain was also in Essex; in Harlow town centre. Another British first was the retail discount store which opened in 1960 as Supa-Save in central Southend. The use of wire trolleys to 'help yourself' was the outcome of visits to the USA in the '50s by the Keddie family, the store's owners. In 1997, the country's first Tesco Extra was opened in Pitsea.

Lakeside Shopping Centre and the adjoining retail park form the largest shopping area in Essex. It has its own chapel and chaplain, a seven-screen multiplex cinema and a 26-acre lake. The retail space totals 1.4 million sq ft, equivalent to seventeen times the surface area of the old Wembley stadium. Lakeside was the first shopping centre to introduce extended weekday opening hours of 10 a.m.–10 p.m. Reputedly, as much as 20 per cent of the population of the UK live within an hour's drive, so it is not that surprising that the Barclays Bank cash dispenser at the centre holds the record for the most amount of money withdrawn in a day in the country. Every week, 450,000 people visit the shops. With 13,000 car parking spaces, there are enough cars to reach from Dover to Calais if parked end to end!

OTHER WAYS TO SPEND SPARE TIME

Playing cards – a pack produced in 1676 had a map of Essex on the back of the seven of hearts with the mileage between Colchester and London and a scale for measuring other distances. In the absence of road maps, this must have been a handy pocket atlas with each card featuring a different county.

Cinema: In 1938, the largest cinema opened in Essex, an Art Deco extravaganza. This was the Grays State cinema, currently planned for a rebirth.

Morris Dancing: Every spring at Thaxted where a Morris Club was started in 1911 by the Revd Conrad Noel. Two to three hundred dancers descend annually in full regalia, and the energetic merriment goes on until late into the evening.

Win a side of pork: In the oldest recorded competition in England, the Dunmow Flitch, dating back to at least 1244, possibly as early as 1104. Every leap year, the couple who can convince judge and jury that they have never once, sleeping or waking, regretted their marriage, are paraded as the winners, as long as they have been married for over a year. (The 'flitch' is another word for the prize joint.)

Join the WI: The Essex Federation of Women's Institutes is the largest WI federation in the country with over 9,500 members in over 230 institutes. That's a lot of calendars.

Paint a picture of Essex: The Victoria & Albert Museum in London, no less, has a number of Essex paintings, apart from those in galleries and museums around the county. The V&A's collection includes 'Interior of the Old Grand Theatre, Colchester' and 'The Cattle Market, Braintree' by Walter Bayes, the 'River Brain, Witham' and 'Waltham Abbey' by H.E. du Plessis, 'The Old Sun Inn, Saffron Walden' and 'The Abbey, Audley End' by William Palmer Robins, and 'St Osyth's Quay' by Rowland Suddaby.

Join a health club: Perhaps you like the idea of the one in Woodford Bridge built on the site of the former Claybury Asylum, a place which accommodated 800 male and 1,200 female pauper 'lunatics' in the nineteenth century. The Asylum's chapel is now the club's swimming pool.

Ice skating: At the only ice rink in Essex, located at Chelmsford, home of the Chieftains Ice Hockey team.

Bird-watching: Perhaps at the only bird-watching fair in the South East which takes place in Waltham Abbey in February spreading across the 1,000-acre Lea Valley Country Park.

FORMER PLEASURES

Sport was actively discouraged when Queen Elizabeth I was on the throne – with the exception of archery. Every father had to give his sons and servants (aged between seven and sixteen) a longbow and two arrows, and every man over seventeen had to own four arrows and a longbow. Additionally, every parish had to provide 'butts' on Sundays for archery practice, and it was a failure to comply with this (for several months) that led to the residents of Purleigh being fined 12 (old) pence each in 1591.

Bull-baiting was openly advertised as taking place at the King's Arms, Burnham, at ten o'clock on 10 October 1783, the master of the best dog to be entitled to a 'gold laced hat'.

Essex managed to beat London in 1769 at the annual cock-fighting competition which took place at Hornchurch and comprised thirty-six bouts, all won by 'Essex gentlemen'.

Ways of celebrating peace (i.e. Napoleon's defeat) at Saffron Walden in 1814 included catching a pig with a soaped tail, and a snuff-taking 'race'. In 1838, the village was celebrating Queen Victoria's coronation with such delights as a bonnet-and-cap race (prize: a bonnet) and a donkey race (prize: a bridle).

The nineteenth century was a popular period for bare-fist prize fighting. Although pronounced illegal in the mid-nineteenth century, knuckle contests still defiantly continued. There was a memorable

AFTER THE FIRST GRIP.

Arth-r B-lf-r (h himself). " I ALWAYS SAID I WANTED A STRONG 'UN, AND, BY JOVE, I RATHER THINK I 'VE FOUND HIM ! "

thirty-five-round match at Canvey Island in 1857, and the last heavyweight competition under prize-ring rules took place between Jem Mace and Tom King in November 1862 at Fobbing. Hundreds of spectators travelled from Fenchurch Street on early-morning trains, paying two sovereigns to watch the match. The contest went the full twenty-one rounds, Tom King being the winner and collecting a prize belt and £300.

Until 1868, there was an annual wrestling competition held in Hornchurch on Christmas Day, with as many as twenty villagers involved. The winner received a boar's head prepared at Hornchurch Hall.

William Kempster from Orsett won the National Quoit Championship of Great Britain in 1895, 1896 and 1911 as well as a host of other titles including the Essex Challenge Cup.

In 1909 and 1911, the last ploughing matches held in the south of England took place at Fairlop Plain, with sixty-nine and seventy-six ploughs taking part respectively.

FACTS FOR SPORTY TYPES

Horse Racing

Galleywood Race Course at Chelmsford can be traced back to the time of George II. It seems that in about 1770 two sons, one pious and one a gambler, inherited money, the first son building a church and the other defiantly building a race-course around it. Thus, Galleywood became the largest in Britain, and the only one to circle a church. It closed in 1935.

Great Leighs racecourse – floodlit, all weather and 'state of the art' opened on 4 April 2008 on the former Essex County Showground.

Cricket

When Kent players turned up in October 1776 to play Essex at Tilbury Fort, there was uproar when one player was recognised as being brought in from 'outside' to play in the Kent team. Legend suggests that the subsequent scuffle resulted in two men dying (the guards at the fort had muskets but were not so good at guarding them) and the Kent men returned to their boats and back across the Thames.

Hornchurch Cricket Club was founded in 1782 and was at one time undefeated for seven years. They managed a draw with the MCC on 10 June 1831.

Only three cricket clubs are allowed to play on forest land in Essex, namely Woodford Green (still playing on its original ground and dating from 1735), Buckhurst Hill and Epping Foresters.

Although Essex County Cricket Club was formed in 1876 at Brentwood, the earliest record of major trophies is over a century later with their 1979 victories in the County Championship and the Benson & Hedges Cup.

The most phenomenal score in the history of British cricket was in August 1882 on Rickling Green. The village team were all out for 94 on day one, but the Orleans Club managed 920 runs on day two.

Herongate Cricket Club, near Brentwood, has the smallest straight boundaries in Essex at just 30 metres.

Go-Karting

Rayleigh Karting claims to be the longest indoor circuit in Essex. The largest (about 1,000 metres) and fastest circuit, however, is at Lakeside, rivalling all other centres in the UK. It offers three circuits and three kart styles.

Football

The oldest football club in Essex is Saffron Walden founded in 1872. They are the twenty-third oldest in the world!

The first seven-a-side football competition to be played in England was organised by Ilford Wanderers in April 1926.

Rugby

The William Webb Ellis trophy, named after the rector of Laver Magdalen (now Magdalen Laver) may have been wrongly attributed. He was alleged to have been the first to run with the ball (result: rugby) and has an international rugby union stadium named after him in Johannesburg as well as being immortalised in the name of the most coveted prize in the game. The story of how football split between Rugby and Association has been hotly disputed since his death in 1872, but it remains a worthy Essex legend.

Southend-on-Sea has the county's oldest rugby club, founded in 1870.

Speedway

The first venue for speedway racing in the UK was at High Beach, near Loughton, dating from February 1928.

Fishing

Billericay and District Angling Club is the largest in the county.

Golf

Frinton Golf Club, founded in 1895, insisted on knee-length socks for its members until July 2008 when the rule was relaxed to allow short socks.

Ballards Gore Golf Club, in Canewdon, has the longest 18-hole parkland course in Essex.

Sailing

Three gold medallists in the sailing events at the London 1908 Olympics were from the Royal Burnham Yacht Club at Burnham-on-Crouch, the same club producing four gold medallists in the 1920 Antwerp Olympics.

Boxing

Georges Carpentier, the French world light-heavyweight boxing champion, came to the UK to fight at Olympia, London, in May 1922, and did his training at the gymnasium at the Shoebury Hotel. He liked to swing a hammer along with the local blacksmith at the latter's hut on the beach – and it seems to have worked, because he (the 'Orchid Man') stopped Kid 'the Aldgate Sphinx' Lewis in the first round.

In March 1987, 5,000 people watched Terry Marsh – the undefeated world light welterweight champion – stop American Joe Marley in round ten in a circus marquee on a car park in Basildon.

Darts

The first player to clock up 200 games for Essex was Sheila Busby from Clacton. In February 2008, Sheila reached the magic milestone with her ninety-seventh victory in twenty-five years, while representing Essex Ladies against Yorkshire.

And here's an Olympic sport with a difference
Reece Price from Wickford, aged just eleven, won the first ever Mobile Phone Olympics in 2003. The event took part on Clapham Common in London, with 10,000 participants proving their skill at picture and text messaging, game playing and mobile phone throwing. Reece managed 80 text characters in 56 seconds, a picture message in 21 seconds, a score of 11,365 points on *Tony Hawks Pro Skater 4*, and a throw of 114ft (35m).

FOR THOSE WHO PREFER DRINKING TO WATCHING (OR JOINING IN)

While there are several claims to being the oldest 'pub' in Essex, the title seems to belong to St Anne's Castle in Great Leighs, which has been mentioned in the Domesday Book and is referred to as supplying ale to twelfth-century pilgrims. The pub is still there, although it has adopted various guises over the years – even as a hermitage at one point.

The Golden Lion in South Street, Romford, was once owned by the Elizabethan Sir Francis Bacon, and, hundreds of years later, was a favourite with Wilfred Owen, the soldier poet who was stationed at Gidea Park before the First World War.

When a Mr Lambert was 'master of The Cock and Bell' at Writtle, near Chelmsford, in 1768, he entered into a 20-mile race – with a horse! The betting was considerable – presumably on the horse – but Mr Lambert returned a half hour before the animal, and, if the *Chelmsford Chronicle* is to be believed, ran his first 10 miles in an amazing 63 minutes.

The Epping Place Inn (now closed) had higher doors than usual to accommodate long-time resident Patrick O'Brien, who alledgedly stood at 8ft 4in. Patrick died aged 37 in 1801 – at the inn.

At the beginning of the twentieth century, there were three pubs near the junction of New Street and Great Square, Braintree. The Three

Tuns was known as Little Hell, The George was known as Great Hell, and The Green Man was known as Damnation!

James Francis, the oldest publican in Essex, worked at The Crown, Hadleigh, until his death in 1935 aged ninety-three.

The smallest pub in Essex is The Cornucopia in Southend-on-Sea, which in the 1950s featured such ornamentation as preserved Siamese twin monkeys and a glass case with stuffed squirrels playing billiards in evening dress. While these are no longer in evidence, the tiny pub still sets trends, hosting an early same-sex wedding ceremony in 2005 between two OAPs.

SEVEN ODD INN NAMES AROUND ESSEX

The Men Found Out opened briefly in 1849, Shoeburyness.

The Case is Altered was an inn at Bradwell.

The Wig and Fidgett at Boxted (which closed in 2005) was named after its builders, Obadiah Wigg and Nathaniel Fidgett.

The Captain Mannering in Shoeburyness sported a picture of Captain Mainwaring(!) from *Dad's Army* until 2009, when the pub was renamed the Garrison Arms.

The Kicking Dicky at Dunmow. Dicky is an old slang term for a donkey.

The House without a Name can be found at Easthorpe.

The Hoy and Helmet (origins probably in 'hoy', a Danish boat, and 'helmet', a primitive jetty) is on the site of the Battle of Benfleet.

9

TRANSPORT ON AND ABOVE THE GROUND

HORSE-POWER

The first carriers (in the sixteenth century) were for goods rather than people, but by the seventeenth century primitive stagecoaches were running daily through such destinations as Barking and Romford. A journey to Colchester from London at this time would take as long as two days. By 1754, the coach services had speeded up, with a commercial service from Chelmsford daily at 7 a.m. There were changes for the horses at the White Hart, Brentwood and the Green Man, Ilford, and the coach arrived at the Bull Inn, Leadenhall Street in London at 12 noon, leaving again at 2 p.m. to be back in Chelmsford by 7 p.m. which was great news for part-timers or London lunchers. Horses were still, of course, used for some 'post' services, and by individual travellers.

The first road repair machine was invented by John Harriott (founder of the Thames River Police) in 1786. The local Essex clay roads were damaged by the heavy wagons which were drawn by up to eight horses, so, as Surveyor of Highways for Great Stambridge, John Harriott came up with a road harrow with spikes which uprooted the mounds and repacked them into ruts. For this inspiration, he won ten guineas from the Society for the Encouragement of the Arts, Manufactures and Commerce in 1789.

The 1836 Directory of Stagecoach Services lists one return coach per day between London and Southend-on-Sea. It left Southend at 7.45 a.m. to reach The Bull at Aldgate in London by 1.45 p.m., arriving back in Southend at 8.45 p.m. after just one hour in the capital. The coach, called The Despatch, carried just four people inside and eleven outside.

Such lengthy stagecoach journeys could be tedious, and Thomas Hood, resident of Lake House, Wanstead, from 1832, enlivened his trip one day by taking a plump female fellow-traveller on to his knee. Imagine Thomas's red face at his destination, when they alighted together – she was his new cook. As a practical joker who illustrated his own comic annuals, Thomas probably made good use of the incident.

At its peak, twenty-five coaches a day stopped at Epping to change horses and the area had twenty public houses to service them.

What seems to have been the earliest speeding offence in Essex was in May 1823 when the drivers of two Colchester stagecoaches were fined £3 7s each for driving 'furiously' at 'the extraordinary rate of fourteen to fifteen mph.' Boy racers are nothing new then.

FROM BUSES . . . TO TRAMS

There is a memorial in Chigwell parish church to George Shillibeer (1779–1866), a local man who invented the horse-drawn omnibus with seats inside and outside, adding to the numbers that could be carried previously by stagecoach. In 1829 he drove the first one, using three horses, along the Marylebone Road to the City of London. The fare for this trip was 1s where the stagecoach charged 2s 6d for the same journey. However, he lost money when the railways came along not much later, but the memorial was erected by 'the Busmen of London as a Token of Respect for the Founder of their Calling.' His name also lives on in Shillibeer Walk, Chigwell Row.

The first female tram driver in Britain was Annie Overton from Leigh-on-Sea. She joined the service as a conductor in 1914, aged just seventeen. At the outbreak of the First World War she volunteered to be a driver, setting a precedent.

THE RAILWAY REVOLUTION

Before Sir John Tyrrell, Baronet of Boreham House near Chelmsford, consented to the new Eastern Counties railway passing through his estate in 1838, he stipulated that by way of partial compensation for damage to his property the company should provide him with a private railway station near to his home. He also insisted that he should have the right to stop any train passing through should he wish to board or alight . . . and the company agreed to his requests! These unique privileges continued for forty years until Sir John's death in September 1877, and the station (or perhaps shed is a better description) was demolished a day or two after his funeral.

The first steam train in Essex ran on 18 June 1839 from Mile End to Romford. However, around forty years earlier, a horse-drawn railway was installed in the chalk pits at Purfleet by Samuel Whitbread, the owner. Lime manufacture was the main industry and the railway provided a sturdy and cost-effective method of moving the chalk from his quarry to ship or barge.

The biggest viaduct in East Anglia, some 80ft high and with thirty-two arches, crosses the River Colne at Chappel. It is the largest that the Great Eastern Railway ever built (1847–9) and used seven million bricks in its construction, although it only carries the railway some 320 yards.

Punch magazine was less impressed with the coming of the railway in Essex. A cartoon in January 1849 drew attention to the inadequacies

of Witham station, and William Makepeace Thackerary is quoted in the magazine (in February 1850) in the form of a lampoon: 'By the Heastern Counties Railway vich the shares I don't desire.' An early disappointed share-holder it seems.

In 1872 a 600-metre track was laid at Buckhurst Hill for experimental runs of a single steam locomotive, christened *The Cintra*. Its two small carriages hauled local school-children up and down to test what was intended as a new tram-way system for Lisbon. Although the experiment was successful and *The Cintra* was shipped at great expense to Portugal, it was never utilised. No doubt it seemed like a good idea at the time.

One of the few railways to remain independent during its lifetime was Corringham Light Railway, one of the smallest public railways in the country at 3 miles long. It was the only railway line to operate without signals, opening in 1901 to ferry workers from Corringham to Kynoch's major ammunition factory at Shell Haven Creek, Coryton, known as Kynochtown. The railway closed in 1952.

Perhaps it's a pity that the original planned name for Westcliff-on-Sea station (Kensington-on-Sea) did not go ahead as planned in 1895 – the idea to attract 'upper class' trippers was a missed marketing opportunity. Langford station (near Maldon) was more pro-active in attracting customers: it advertised itself in 1910 as the 'only station in England with a station master.'

There were 1,750 shunting horses still in service with the Great Eastern Railway in 1911. The horses – referred to as Class GG (gee-gee . . . get it?) – had fodder prepared for them at a Romford factory, and were all branded on their forefeet. GER must have been one of the biggest horse-owners in the county, if not the country.

Up, Up and Away

It was a French aeronaut (i.e. balloonist) who was the first to land on Essex soil. Jean Pierre Blanchard landed at Laindon Hills in May 1785, having started his flight in London.

The first recorded Essex man to take to the skies was George Rush from Elsenham Hall. His balloon took off from Vauxhall Gardens in London (with two companions) on 4 September 1838, and reached 19,000ft.

The first balloon crossing of the North Sea was made in 1883 by Sir Claude Champion de Crespigny who had been living at Champion Lodge (later Totham Lodge) at Great Totham since 1881. An ex-army and ex-navy man, he landed successfully in Flushing, Holland, having taken off from Maldon. His companion on this flight was Joseph Simmons; both men had several failed attempts prior to 1883.

Three 1888 pioneers, who were ambitiously en route from the Olympia Exhibition in London to Vienna, abandoned their plan because of the unfavourable weather when over Ulting, near Maldon. They identified a barley field suitable for landing, but the grappling iron they threw out failed to connect and became entangled in a tree. As a result, the balloon hit the ground, bounced and burst. Their plight was witnessed by locals from Hatfield Peverel and Woodham Walter. Joseph Simmons – Sir Claude's companion in 1883 – died at the scene, and the other two adventurers were both badly injured.

Horatio Phillips, a Southminster landowner, devised a multi-plane mounted on a set of bicycle wheels with a tiny petrol engine, which he claims flew a few feet from the ground for a distance of over 20 yards in September, 1903; but there were no witnesses to what would have been a remarkable aviation first. His twenty-storey contraption can be seen in the opening sequence of *Those Magnificent Men in their Flying Machines*.

Essex can claim a part in the first powered flight at Kitty Hawk, North Carolina, in 1903 because the Wright Brothers were descended directly from Samuel Wright of Kelvedon Hall, near Brentwood, who left for a new life in Boston in the seventeenth century. It also seems that one of the students of the Wright Brothers (Robert Mackfie), on arriving in England, briefly stored his plane in the grounds of the Kursaal at Southend-on-Sea, grounds now covered with housing.

Dagenham Lake (or, more accurately, Dagenham Breach as it was originally known) was the site of the first organised flight ground in the country. It was opened by the Royal Aeronautical Society in 1909 for prospective aviators but failed to produce any successful attempts at flying during its first year and was later abandoned.

The first Essex pilot to qualify for his aviator's certificate was Edward Petre of Ingatestone on 24 July 1912. He had passed all his flying tests at Fairlop.

In 1913, Bentfield 'Benny' Hucks, born at Stansted Mountfitchet in 1884, was the first British pilot to perform a loop-the-loop (at Hendon).

Amy Johnson was taught to fly by Captain Froude R. Matthews from Southend-on-Sea in 1928, qualifying in 1929. There is a record of her flying from Stapleford Tawney (known as Essex Airport) to Paris on 24 August 1934. When Amy was ferrying airplanes from factories to RAF bases for the Air Transport Auxiliary in 1941, she crashed in low cloud into the Thames Estuary at Foulness. Her body was never recovered, although a wing from her Oxford was washed up at Shoebury Beach three days later.

Edward Hillman's air passenger service from Maylands Farm, Harold Wood, the first in Essex, only operated for twelve years (from 1932), but had a profound effect on modern commercial aviation. It was the first aerodrome to offer charter flights to destinations like Clacton, Margate and Norwich; it ran the first air mail service to Scotland and Northern Ireland, and in 1933 it operated the first scheduled flights – twice daily in the summer – from 'London' to Paris. Hillman,

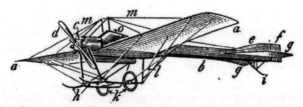

Aëroplane. *a, a* Supporting Planes; *b* Fuselage; *c* Engine; *d* Propeller; *e* Vertical Plane; *f* Rudder; *g, g* Elevating Planes; *h* Landing Skids; *i* Tail Skid; *k* Wheels; *l* Warping Wires; *m* Stays; *o* Aviator's Compartment.

from Romford, offered a lower fare (£5 10s) and a shorter flight time than his only rival, Imperial Airways. This pioneering story had an unhappy ending – all Maylands aircraft and hangars were destroyed in 1940 by German incendiary bombs.

STANSTED STATS

Stansted Airport officially opened in 1991 on the site of a late Iron Age and middle Bronze Age settlement. The remains of nine roundhouses occupied by the Celts between 75 and 25 BC were found where the main parking apron is now.

The airport started life as a USAAF base in 1943 but the public enquiry into its development didn't take place until 1984, taking 258 days and using 38 tons of paper. The enquiry was looking into an increase from 500,000 passengers to a potential 15,000,000.

The first aircraft to attempt to land at Stansted Airfield was an RAF Stirling. It was returning from Nuremburg to Suffolk on 26 February 1943, running low on fuel, but, as the runways were incomplete and obstructed, the aircraft overshot and hit a thicket of trees. The Stirling was destroyed, but it seems the crew escaped without serious injuries.

Stansted's hangar is the only diamond-shaped construction of its kind in the UK and is modelled on Miami's TWA hangar. It also has the world's largest curtain rail to separate the two halves of the hangar.

In the new terminal building (in 1991) an episode of *Songs of Praise* was filmed, with a congregation of 1,500 people from churches within an 8-mile radius – plus a choir of 450.

Instead of the elaborate flypast planned for the queen's opening (15 March 1991) which was due to feature different types of aircraft to represent the history of aviation, a single Harrier took centre stage as a result of the Gulf Crisis.

The largest group of passengers handled at one time at Stansted was 10,000 Italian and Spanish football fans en route to the European Cup Final at Wembley on 14 May 1992. Barcelona beat Sampdoria 1–0 in extra time.

The site covers 213 acres, roughly 10 per cent having been landscaped with a quarter of a million trees and shrubs and 30,000 plants. About 70 acres are sewn with wild flowers and 148 acres have been allocated for new woodlands. The area produces a massive 550 tons of cut grass and weeds every year.

THE MIGHTY MOTOR

The first vehicle built on Henry Ford's innovative moving assembly line at Dagenham from 1931 was the Ford 8hp Model Y, setting Ford-UK on the way to market leadership. It was their first truly small car, their cheapest-ever car, and it opened up Ford motoring to the masses. It ousted the Model T (the first to be offered in any colour 'as long as it is black') produced first in Detroit (from 1908) and then in Manchester.

The arrival of Ford must have been quite a blow to one Thomas Clarkson of Chelmsford who had been working on a light steam car since 1902.

A 20hp Rolls-Royce, owned by Mrs Wythes of Copped Hall, Epping, was sold to her chauffeur in 1929 so that he could set up a car hire business locally. The very same car was offered back to Copped Hall in 2005, where restoration of the house and gardens is ongoing.

In 1933, the main attraction for the summer season at the Kursaal in Southend-on-Sea was Al Capone's car – a green V8 Cadillac, with steel armour plating and bullet-proof windows. A sawn-off shotgun was attached to the steering wheel, and the car was fitted with Chicago police broadcast sets and a siren to ensure speedy getaways.

The first traffic wardens appointed in Essex were on 1 April 1964. Note the relevance of 1 April.

Some of the road networks have been immortalised in song. Billy Bragg (the Bard of Barking) has written about the A13 ('the A-road, the OK road'). In a different vein, Chris Rea has sung about 'The Road to Hell' – the M25.

The Queen Elizabeth II Bridge across the River Thames from Thurrock to Dartford in Kent was built at a cost of £184 million, the longest cable-stayed bridge of its kind in Europe, and the third longest in the world, with a total length of about 1.78 miles. It was opened in October 1991.

In April 2005, the number plate F1 was put up for sale by Essex County Council at Bonham's auction house, but failed to reach its reserve, thought to be over £350,000.

Later the same year, it was revealed in the local press that, despite raising £14 million from speeding fines in one five-year period alone, one-third of the speed cameras in Essex are dummies.

10

DEATH AND RELIGION

Unexpected Suicides

Widowed Prudence ffenn hung herself the day after her second marriage, which took place on the 15 August 1592. She is described in the parish register at Little Clacton as a 'most accursed creature' who had 'hanged her selfe' resulting in her burial 'out of the compas of Christian buriall' (*sic*).

On 12 February 1935, sisters Jane and Elizabeth Coert du Bois, aged just twenty and twenty-three, jumped out of a private aeroplane over Upminster. They had been travelling from Stapleford Tawney airport to Paris, following the news that their respective fiancés had been killed in an RAF flying-boat accident. The pilot didn't notice their absence until he was halfway to his destination, and flew back to Essex in a state of shock.

Deadly Data

In 1321, the first Rector of Bradwell-on-Crouch was appointed by the Bishop of London, who chose Imbertus de Monte Martino from Burgundy. The villagers were extremely hostile and, although Imbertus escaped, his brother and sister-in-law were both killed in an angry confrontation. Ten local men were arrested and convicted, but were all pardoned, and this was the last straw for Imbertus, who returned to his homeland.

By 1663, John Pell, the Rector of Laindon, had replaced six curates in sixteen years when, one after the other, they succumbed to malaria. Laindon became known as 'kill priest country' as a result, although Pell also lost his wife, servants and grandchildren to the disease.

A third of Braintree's residents died, as did nearly half of the *c.* 10,000 population of Colchester in 1665 as a result of bubonic plague. Essex was worse affected than any other county, and contemporary cures – saffron (grown locally) or human and animal excrement for instance – had no effect.

In the nineteenth century, Reverend Canon Irvine, the Rector of St Mary's-at-the Walls in Colchester, lost a brother as the result of a cheetah bite. Blame could perhaps be laid at the door of the Maharajah of Vizianagram who had been 'entertaining' the young man at the time.

Rettendon Windmill had claimed two victims by 1853. The first was three-year-old Elizabeth Jefferies who wandered too close to the low sails, and the other was George Borrodell who was pushing a wheelbarrow which slowed his ability to escape the downward swish in good time.

The Revd Thomas Byles of St Helen's Church, Ongar, booked his passage to New York to officiate at the wedding of his brother – in April 1912. Sadly, he changed his original booking to an earlier one, travelling on the maiden voyage of the *Titanic*. Before his tragic end, he was able to offer absolution and the last rites to his similarly-doomed fellow travellers.

When the rector of St Clement's, West Thurrock, opened a 1723 coffin during renovations in 1906, he was stunned to find the body of Nathaniel Grantham (a sailor) preserved, appropriately, in rum. It seems Nathaniel had died on the water but did not want to be buried at sea, and this was the best way of preserving the body until it could be buried in the soil.

When recovering a dead man's body at Jaywick following the 1953 floods, the book discovered open on the table of the man's house was: *The Cruel Sea.*

BONES AND ASHES

When William Book of Dagenham died in 1433, his will provided for a sheep to be driven before his body on the day of his burial, a fairly common practice in Essex.

The largest tomb in the grounds of St Giles and All Saints' Church, Orsett, belongs to generations of the Bonham family, with special mention of Captain Samuel Bonham, the wealthy owner of Orsett House who died in 1745. It doesn't say, however, that he made a lot of his money from the slave trade, slaves being just one commodity he transported from Africa to the Caribbean. In just one trip, in 1733 on the *Sarah Galley,* along with the gold and the elephant tusks, he arrived with 167 slaves although 408 started the journey.

A miserly tinker from Hornchurch, one Edward No(a)kes, was opposed to an extravagant funeral – although he didn't mind spending money on a quart 'of spirits' every day. He ordered that his coffin should be made without nails, using a cord as fastening, and that the pall (coffin-cover) should be made from an old sheet rather than the traditional velvet. He left 2s 6d to pay the coffin-bearers, and £6,000 (a fortune in 1802) to his wife and family, with instructions that no one should wear mourning at his funeral – even the undertaker turned up in blue coat and red waistcoat.

The lock-up at Foulness, originally erected for wrong-doers, was tried out as a mortuary in the mid-nineteenth century, but the full-length bodies were too long to fit into the available space, meaning that the feet protruded outside. Not surprisingly, the trial was discontinued.

A Maori 'Prince' (an honorary title) named Moki, a private in the New Zealand Expeditionary Forces and son of the ruling chief of Nieu, died in the convalescent home of Grey Towers in Hornchurch in 1916. His remains are in St Andrew's graveyard.

In 2001, archaeologists found evidence of syphilis in the skeleton of a young woman buried at St Mary and All Saints in Rivenhall. The significance of the discovery lies in the fact that she died before 1445, fifty years before Columbus travelled to the New World. Until then, Columbus had been 'blamed' for the introduction of syphilis to Europe.

The first green burial ground, a natural alternative to traditional graveyards and crematoria, was opened in 1996 at Wrabness, Manningtree, overlooking the Stour Estuary. More recently (2007) a woodland site was opened at Epping Forest. This site covers 52 acres and cost £2.7 million to complete. One of its earliest, and very well-attended, services was in honour of the zany Ken Campbell, the Ilford actor.

Archaeologists at Stanway in April 2008 made the first discovery in Britain of a druid grave. The team uncovered the earliest surgical equipment ever found, including a scalpel and saw, plus some jet (believed to have been magical), a board game with glass counters, and the remains of a herbal brew.

INTRIGUING MEMORIALS

The chest-tomb of Mary Ellis in St Clement's churchyard, Leigh-on-Sea, is inscribed with her description as a virgin with 'virtuous courage and very promising hopes who died the 3rd day of June 1609 aged 119.' She could well be the oldest virgin that Essex has ever known. The tomb is often referred to as the 'cutlass tomb' because of the gashes in the stone which could well be from smugglers and press gangs sharpening their cutlasses.

There is a monument to Dame Mary Honywood at St Peter-ad-Vincula at Coggeshall, who died in 1620 aged ninety-three. Of her sixteen children, thirteen reached adulthood, and she left 367 descendants behind her. She is less well known for her support for the Marian Martyrs.

In 1888, a memorial stained-glass window was erected in the north aisle of St Mary's Church, Saffron Walden, in honour of John Thomas Frye. He was an organist at the church from 1824 until 1884, being appointed at just eight years of age. It seems this memorial will soon be joined by another, to Cyril Coe, who, similarly, was deputy organist from 1947 (aged twelve) until 2007.

All Saints' Church at Brightlingsea has a frieze of over 200 ceramic tiles to mark the names of all locals lost at sea since 1872. The names include those who died aboard the *Titanic*.

Ten Essex Ghosts

Coggeshall is haunted by the ghost of a sixteenth-century woodcutter called Robin. The blows of his ghostly axe have often been heard, and the local brook is known as Robin's Brook in his memory.

Colchester lays claim, among others, to the ghost of several former Roman soldiers. One is said to haunt the police station built on a Roman burial site; others have been 'seen' in the vicinity of The Old Anchor.

Cressing Temple – site of the first Knights Templar in England – has more than one ghost on offer. The most convincing is the Hall Man, seen a few times since the 1970s, appearing at the top of the main staircase with large hat and long curly hair.

Great Wakering has a ghost in the shape of Clement the Baker. The road junction where he has been spotted lies near to the site of his burial following suicide. It is known locally as Baker's Grave.

Maldon was the home of John Gates, beheaded for his involvement in the Lady Jane Grey plot (1553). He lived at Beeleigh Abbey and his headless ghost is said to appear regularly every year on the anniversary of his death (22 August).

Mistley is the site of The Thorn Hotel, famously haunted by one-time resident Matthew Hopkins, the Witchfinder General himself. Perhaps the torture and evil he did in life that made him 'stink in men's nostrils' has prevented his spirit from resting.

Snaresbrook is the location of ghostly sightings of a rider along the Woodford Road. The area was once notorious for its highway robberies, and the rider is said to be one such victim, Sir Caesar Child, who died in the mid-eighteenth century.

South Weald near Brentwood has a rather famous ghost – Lord Byron no less. The poet was a frequent visitor to his friends the Hanson family, who lived at Gilstead Hall (formerly Wealdside). Why he should return to haunt the grounds after his death is, of course, yet another mystery.

Stock has an unusual ghost in the form of a pub landlord called Charlie 'Spider' Marshall, who died in the chimney of The Bear Inn. It seemed he liked to spend time in the chimney, but no-one knows why – he usually came out if a fire was lit, but not on the last occasion. Perhaps his charred remains are still there?

Upminster's Golf Club (previously Havering Hall) is haunted by the ghost of a young woman in white. She is said to have been the victim of a previous owner who kidnapped her when she refused his advances and bricked her up in a tiny room to die.

A FEW GRISLY EVENTS

Over fifty Essex Protestants, a higher proportion than any other region of England, were put to death during the reign of Bloody Mary. One such victim, in 1555, was nineteen-year-old William Hunter, burned to death in Brentwood. His remains were left alongside the elm tree that had acted as a stake. His crime? Reading the Bible in English. Ironically, three years later, one of the magistrates who had condemned him to such a horrific execution, local squire Sir Anthony Browne of Weald Hall, went on to found Brentwood School for Boys – to teach 'virtue, learning and manners.' The Martyr's Elm remains as a grim reminder of the dangers of religious fanaticism.

In 1854, John Scrivener of Bradfield, the local blacksmith, was preparing to celebrate his marriage in the usual fashion of his profession at the time – by blowing up his anvil. By choosing a sledge-hammer to force the gunpowder home, however, he caused an explosion which drove the handle of the hammer right through his body, killing him instantly.

ABBEYS AND PRIORIES, MONASTERIES AND CONVENTS

The monks of the twelfth-century Augustinian Thoby Priory, Mountnessing, were needed to meet the local demand for available men when the women-folk were deserted for lengthy periods of time (their men-folk busy at the Crusades or elsewhere). The introduction of Leap Day was seemingly instituted to allow some of these desperate women to propose marriage just once every four years. As acceptance of such a proposal could not be binding (by 'law') if the man was drunk, the monks brewed up liquor for the event, christened Old Trouser Leg Shaker, to ensure they were not sober.

Robber Baron John Fitzwalter was involved in a feud with the Priory of Dunmow in 1351. He eventually abducted eighteen cows and one bull belonging to the priory and drove them to Woodham Walter where they starved to death after being compounded.

In 1381, John of Gaunt paid £50 to Barking Abbey for novitiate fees of Elizabeth Chaucer, believed to be Geoffrey Chaucer's daughter.

1519 was the year Henry Fitzroy, illegitimate son of Henry VIII, was born at the twelfth-century St Laurence's Priory at Blackmore, near Brentwood. The king's young mistress, Elizabeth 'Bessie' Blount, was not quartered with the holy men, but allowed the use of the prior's main residence nearby. Cardinal Wolsey made all the arrangements, and, by choosing a priory rather than a nunnery, he may have reduced the chances of gossip. The village stream was once known as The Jordan, and, when Henry VIII went to visit Bessie, he told the court he was 'going to Jericho.'

The last abbot of St John's, Colchester, John Beche, was hanged from the abbey gateway in 1539 after refusing to surrender the abbey keys, and for daring to question the authority of Henry VIII.

In 2004, a major excavation in the grounds of Prittlewell Priory (Southend-on-Sea) revealed the burial chamber of a Saxon king, probably Saebba. This was the most important Saxon find to date in Essex, throwing light on the little known seventh century. The remains of the 'King of Bling' – so called because of the gold, silver and bronze artefacts buried with him – are temporarily at the Museum of London until they can be rehoused in Southend.

Seven Saints' Days Connected to Essex

18 August: St Helen was born in Colchester in about AD 250. The legend suggests that she was a) the daughter of King Coel (or Cole) and b) the mother of the Roman Emperor Constantine. She is credited with finding Christ's Cross (on Mount Calvary) and is the Patron Saint of Colchester and of Archaeologists.

3 September: St Constantine, the Roman Emperor, was supposedly the son of St Helen and Constantius. He became the first Christian Emperor of Rome, on 25 May AD 306, while serving in Britain.

7 October: St Osyth was the daughter of Frithwald, a ruler of Mercia. She vowed perpetual virginity but was betrothed against her will to

the King of the East Saxons (Sighere). Whether the marriage was consummated or not is unclear, but Sighere gifted Osyth with enough land to build a nunnery. In AD 653 the Danes beheaded her during their sackings, and many believe that she picked up her head and walked three furlongs to the church where she fell to the ground. As a result, a fountain sprung up at the site of this event and the water was renowned for its restorative property.

11 October: St Ethelburgh was the sister of the Bishop of London (Erkenwald) who appointed her in about AD 670 as the first Abbess of Barking nunnery, the first 'monastery for women' in England. After an austere life, this is where she was buried in 687.

26 October: St Cedd, a missionary who landed at Bradwell-on-Sea in about AD 643, built St Peter's Chapel. The King of the Northumbrians wanted Cedd to convert the East Saxons, and, as Bishop of the East Saxons, Cedd did a good job. But when he died of yellow fever in his forties, many converts believed this was a sign that the old pagan gods were offended by what they had done, and promptly reverted to paganism. He remains the Patron Saint of Essex.

14 November: St Erkenwald, Bishop of London from AD 675 until his death, gave up his share of family money to establish a Benedictine abbey at Barking and another at Chertsey (Surrey), serving as abbot of the latter. He was the first bishop to preach in St Paul's Cathedral, London.

20 November: St Edmund, crowned King of the East Angles at Bures St Mary on 25 December 855, was killed fourteen years later in a battle with the Danes. When his body was found, it was without the head which had been thrown into the forest, but Edmund's supporters found it by virtue of the head calling 'here I am' to assist them in their search. Although his body (with head now mysteriously but firmly attached) was finally buried in what is now Bury St Edmunds, Greensted Church was the site of an overnight stay for his body on his final journey (in about 1013), and there is a window there dedicated to St Edmund. He remains the Patron Saint of East Anglia.

BELIEVERS WITH A DIFFERENCE

Richard Farnham, a Colchester weaver, had persuaded some deluded souls that he was a prophet who could save them from the end of the world. He persuaded one Mrs Haddington that she was actually married to him, which she believed (although her husband was at sea), landing them both in prison. She was released into the custody of her husband, but Farnham, also released, died of the plague in January 1641. Mrs Haddington and his other followers were very puzzled when Farnham did not rise from the grave as expected. Only then did she realise her own foolishness.

The Tillingham virgin mother, Mary Adams, who gave birth to a misshapen 'monster' in about 1652, allegedly the child of the Holy Ghost, is likely to be a complete fiction. The pamphlet about her, *The Ranter's Monster*, seems to have been more of a warning against licentiousness than an embodiment of fact. The Ranters themselves were a free-thinking sect that believed that God created the entire world, good and bad, without a devil or hell, and that life was for living, including 'free love'. If there was a Mary Adams, then it is this lifestyle that is to blame for her 'unexpected' (?) pregnancy although not for the baby's disability.

A Christian sect unique to South Essex was started in the 1830s by James Banyard from Rochford, a reformed poacher. He set up the Peculiar People (i.e. God's chosen people, from Deuteronomy), a religion based on elemental Methodism which believes there is no sin in Christians or doubt in believers. They believed in divine healing without medical intervention, and the sect split when Banyard called out a doctor for his sick son in 1855 and so lost his credibility and his leadership.

Rodney or 'Gypsy' Smith, from a Wanstead gypsy family, became an evangelist at the Salvation Army Mission in London in 1877. It was the first time he had lived in a room rather than a tent, and his magnificent singing contributed to his influence in converting thousands of others both here and in the USA and Australia.

Manningtree station, 15 February 1909, was the scene for a struggle between a novitiate nun (Dame Maurus, otherwise known as

Margaret Moult), two sisters from East Bergholt Abbey, the driver of their trap, and the station porters. Margaret had decided that the religious life was not for her and made a run for it on a rainy night, with the nuns in hot pursuit in their 'wagonette'. The station was where they caught up with the bedraggled, muddy runaway, but the porters, and then the station master, were sympathetic to the screaming nun who was holding on to a fence in a desperate attempt to avoid being returned to the awful conditions in the convent. She was put on to a train to return to her family in London, and, because the escape hit the headlines, made the most of the situation by writing a book about her adventures, which became a best-seller.

FIFTEEN INFLUENTIAL CHURCHMEN

Between 1615 and 1635 the Revd Gilbert Dillingham of Sandon, near Chelmsford, performed 511 quickie weddings. He had effectively set up a kind of Essex Gretna Green and charged accordingly. A nice little earner for his retirement.

The Rector of Purleigh from 1632 to 1643 was Laurence Washington, the great-great-grandfather of the first president of the USA. Two of his sons emigrated to America, unhappy with local Royalist activities, and it was John who became George Washington's great-grandfather. When the fourteenth-century Purleigh Church was restored in 1892, it was grateful American money that paid for the major works.

An early graffiti nuisance was the Revd Samuel Purchas Junior, the seventeenth-century rector of Sutton (north of Southend). He scratched his name and date (1642) on the jamb of a window in the chancel of the parish church of St Andrew (Rochford), on the panelling in the porch at Sutton Church, and on a bedroom door taken from the Old Rectory at Sutton on its subsequent demolition.

The first Minister of Maldon congregational chapel from 1696 was Joseph Billio. Such was his enthusiasm and the fervour of his sermons that his name has been attributed to the word billyo (extreme) now in the English language. As the word was not popularised until much later, this may not be the truth, but, as so often the case, there is no evidence to the contrary.

When the Revd Robert Houlton gave a sermon on the benefits of inoculation against smallpox on 12 October 1766 at Ingatestone, he was not to know that Daniel Sutton, who carried out the inoculations, was to become very wealthy as a result.

Sir Henry Bate Dudley of Bradwell-on-Sea (1745–1824) earned the name the 'fighting parson' after taking part in two duels. The first (with pistols) was in defence of alleged libel against the Countess of Strathmore, and the second (with fists) was a protest against slanderous remarks about a Mrs Hartley. Not averse to taking sides, he was also involved in the East Anglian riots caused by poverty exacerbated by the return of soldiers after the Napoleonic Wars. Sir Henry actively assisted in the quelling of the 'Littleport Riots' near Cambridge and was rewarded with a gold cup and a silver plate for his efforts.

The vicar of Southminster achieved fame by accompanying Nelson on his conquering campaigns on HMS *Victory*. Dr Alexander Scott was chaplain and secretary, comforting the Admiral as he lay dying at the Battle of Trafalgar (21 October 1805). He brought back some souvenirs from the ship – a chart table, mirror and bureau – which were passed on to the church (St Leonard's).

Although Baptist Charles Haddon Spurgeon (1834–92) resisted early pressure to train for the ministry, at his peak he attracted larger congregations than anyone else in Essex and beyond. One of seventeen children, he spent his childhood in Kelvedon, Stambourne and Colchester, but was preaching in London while still a teenager. At the time of the Indian Mutiny, 24,000 went to hear him talk at the Crystal Palace, and regular crowds of between seven and ten thousand attended the Metropolitan Tabernacle, known for a while as Spurgeon's Chapel. His popularity can be judged by the sales of his 3,500 sermons; they sold between 25,000 and 30,000 copies at 1d each.

Between 1871 and 1881, while Rector of St Edmunds, East Mersea, the Revd Sabine Baring-Gould wrote a number of books featuring the local area as his backdrop. His most famous work was *Mehalah*, but, far more famously, he was also responsible for writing – allegedly overnight – 'Onward Christian Soldiers', still a popular hymn today. Interestingly, the British Library had more of his booklets and novels than any other writer for a while, as his final total came close to 150; this in addition to hundreds of articles, poems, hymns and pamphlets.

An Irish-born curate with a speech impediment made quite an impression at St Mary's, Prittlewell (Southend), from 1822. This was Frederick Nolan, who did not take kindly to being woken as early as 5 a.m. by the bell-ringing, and, when the bell-ringers refused to change their custom, promptly cut the bell ropes with a carving knife. He then involved the local constable in preventing the ringers from entering the church, so they broke windows and stoned the rectory, resulting in his progressing from a knife to a pistol. In spite of this, he actually remained in the post for an impressive forty-two years, although an annual anti-Nolan effigy was burned on 5 November for some time.

The Minister of Romford from 1826 was Samuel Hanna Carlisle, who had the body of his young son (who had been drowned) disinterred from his grave, embalmed and kept in his hall for fear of body snatchers.

Thomas Archer, the busy curate – variously – of North Benfleet, Rawreth, Canvey Island, Southchurch and Foulness, around the

turn of the nineteenth century, was known as the 'huntin', shootin', fishin' rector'. This was not surprising given his fondness for fist-fighting, clay-pipe smoking, and his habit of tying his hunter to the church gate, wearing scarlet under his surplice, so no time was wasted between services and hunting.

The Rector of Bradwell-on-Sea from 1904 to 1921 was John Robert Blayney Owen. Born in 1848, he was the first ever international footballer from the area, capped on 7 March 1874 for England in the third ever international match.

The socialist Lady Warwick appointed Conrad Noel the vicar of Thaxted Church in 1921, but he went further than even she had expected. He hung the flags of Sinn Féin and of communism alongside the flag of St George, which caused some local dissent. A man of diverse interests, this vicar also started the annual Morris dancing event in the village.

The Revd Joseph Waddington Graves, the first Canadian soldier to be ordained in khaki, arrived in Dagenham in 1930. He had what you could describe as an irreligious background – store detective, bronco buster, medium for a professional hypnotist and captain in the Canadian forces. As minister of Osborne Hall in Braintree, he persuaded Pipe Major Douglas Taylor to teach some of the enthusiastic Sunday School girls the bagpipes, although Taylor was a tad reluctant to take on girls; little did he know the history he'd be making, especially in Dagenham.

CHURCH CHAT

St Alban's Church, Romford, has a 25ft by 25ft ceiling mural, painted by Mark Cazalet, which includes such secular content as a white van man, Essex girls dancing round their handbags in white stilettos, and greyhounds in race livery (Romford greyhound stadium was nearby).

The parish church of Bulphan St Mary (near Romford) has a stained-glass window which was funded as a result of an innovative idea by the Revd T.A. Teitelbaum, who asked every Mary he could locate in the UK and overseas for 1s. This money, raised between 1903 and 1908, paid for the window, which represents Mary – of course – with Jesus in her arms.

There is a walking stick in the United Reformed Church at Chipping Ongar which David Livingstone used on his many walks to London when he was living in a room there (1840). He was accepted as a probationer by the London Missionary Society along with other students who lived in what are now called Livingstone Cottages. There is a record of his 'drying' in the pulpit at Stanford Rivers during a sermon, and scurrying from the church, which must have been something of a black mark against him. The long, 50-mile walks provided good training for the 4,000 miles he would eventually achieve in Africa, where he died in 1873.

The largest church in Essex is St Mary the Virgin in Saffron Walden, nearly 200ft long. It also has the tallest spire in the county, its peak over 190ft from the ground.

The oldest wooden church to survive in England is at Greensted-juxta-Ongar – it has a claim to have the oldest wooden walls in England, to be the oldest wooden building in Europe, and the oldest wooden church in the world, dating back to the beginning of the eleventh century.

Woodham Walter church was one of only six in the country built in the reign of Queen Elizabeth I, and the only one in Essex. Local research has produced evidence of its being the oldest purpose-built Church of England place of worship in the world.

The first Christian chapel in Essex was founded at St Peter on the Wall, Bradwell, in AD 654. It was built on the foundations of the Roman fort of Othona, and is a very isolated, peaceful spot.

The original parish church of Walton on the Naze was lost to the sea in 1798 as a result of coastal erosion.

St Martin's Church, Basildon, has Europe's first glass bell tower. It was built to celebrate the millennium, but not used in case the glass broke.

The only Art Nouveau church interior in the world can be seen at the Church of St Mary the Virgin, Great Warley. It is Grade I listed, with features including a mother-of-pearl frieze.

11

NATURAL HISTORY

GOING BACK A BIT

Humans first appeared in Essex approximately 400,000 years ago – in the Clacton area. Nearby, the cliffs of the Naze at Walton are world-famous for their fossils. Not quite as old are the 300,000-year-old remains of monkeys, bears, elephants and hippos that have been unearthed at Mersea Island. More recently, in 1964, skeletons of an elephant and an early mammoth were discovered in a clay pit at Aveley which were believed to be 150,000 years old. Elephants also featured in the ceremonial entry of Claudius and the Romans into Colchester – as did camels – in AD 43.

Because stone does not occur naturally in Essex it has to be imported. Similarly, there are no natural lakes in the county – many of the existing lakes were once gravel pits.

In 1880, the Essex Field Club recorded in its 'transactions' that they had a day elephant hunting. The assumption has to be that they

were looking for bones rather than living specimens, because when the Natural History Museum opened in London in 1881, most of the prehistoric animal remains exhibited were from Ilford. Some 100 mammoths and 77 woolly rhinos were on display, donated by Sir Antonio Brady, an amateur geologist. The donations included a mammoth skull, complete with tusks 8ft 8in long, which was over 100,000 years old, and the first such specimen ever found in Britain. Some 300 elephants were uncovered altogether from what became known as the Ilford Elephant Ground.

ESSEX WEATHER

Great Wakering has featured in the *Guinness Book of Records* as the driest place in England with an average annual rainfall of under 20in.

While the 1953 floods in East Anglia – and especially the loss of life on Canvey Island – are still within living memory, and have oft been written about, these are not the first serious floods recorded. The first Essex flood mentioned in writing was in AD 31 but there is an account of a serious flood in the Vange area (near Basildon) in 1620 when Dutch engineers (so pro-active in the reclaiming of marshes from Dagenham to Canvey) were called in to assist. Later, local newspapers give accounts of floods in the summer of 1888 in the area, and again in November 1897 on 'Black Monday'.

Freak weather conditions are nothing new, global warming or no global warming. There was a freak tempest in Chelmsford in June 1774, with, according to the *Chelmsford Chronicle*, 'oak cleaving thunderbolts' threatening to 'strike flat the thick rotundity of the world.' A century later (1879) the coldest night in Essex records was an incredible -21°C in Aveley on 7 February. 1888 has gone down as the year without a summer due to gales in May and snow in July in, for example, Romford and Stock. In June 1897 there was a hailstorm at Ingatestone which was so bad that fish were blown out of ponds and small animals were killed by the stones, some of which were 6in in circumference. More recently, 'the hurricane' came to Essex (and elsewhere) in October 1987, doing serious damage to property and trees across large swathes of the county.

When the 1953 floods devastated the Essex and East Anglia coastline, the HQ of flood relief operations was The Red Cow on Canvey Island, the most seriously affected area with the loss of fifty-eight lives when the sea-wall collapsed. It was chosen for its (relatively) high position on the island, and half a million sandbags were filled from its forecourt during rescue operations. As a result, the pub was renamed The King Canute.

The Essex Earthquake

The most serious natural calamity to strike Essex in comparatively recent history – apart from the 1953 floods – was the earthquake that struck Colchester and the surrounds on 22 April 1884. This was the strongest earthquake to strike the British mainland, measuring 5.1 on the Richter scale, and damaging over 1,250 buildings. The shocks were felt over a 150-mile radius, covering some 50 square miles. In just a few seconds in Peldon, near its epicentre, every single building was damaged in some way. The church turrets at Wivenhoe collapsed, and Langenhoe Church was also badly damaged. Perhaps surprisingly, given the scale of destruction, very few lives were lost.

Doggy Stories

It seems that, in 1733, Bishop Benjamin Petre was saved from robbers by his dog beneath the lime trees at Ingatestone Hall. The hall still exists, and is still lived in, and the ghost of the dog is said to have patrolled the walkway ever since.

Even more unlikely is the story that the Shaen family from Crix, Hatfield Peverel (1770–1858), had a fierce, fire-breathing black dog that could reduce intruders to a pile of hot ashes. Rather more than a guard dog then!

Sir Thomas Barrett-Lennard of Belhus, near Aveley, liked to keep a larger than average number of pet dogs around him at the turn of the twentieth century. When they died, each dog was placed in a coffin and granted a solemn Anglican funeral, complete with prayers read by Sir Thomas. They were then buried in the canine cemetery he had laid out especially in the grounds of Belhus.

The bronze medal of the National Canine Defence League (the 'Victoria Cross') was awarded to a Great Dane from Doddinghurst. Bruce saved his mistress, Mrs Davis, from an attack by a savage boar in June 1934.

Bruce, an Essex police dog, was in the news in 1979 when he made veterinary history. After breaking his natural teeth during training, he was fitted with rust-proof, nickel-chromium fangs – the first doggy dentures.

The Essex Dog Display Team is renowned as the premier dog team in Europe. They are the only civilian dog display team ever selected to appear at the Royal Tournament (in 1997) in front of the queen and other members of the royal family.

The shortest (in height) dog in the world, according to the 2006 *Guinness Book of Records,* is a Yorkshire terrier from Shoeburyness. Whitney was measured at 3in from ground to shoulder, half the height of a Chihuahua.

AND SOME CATTY TALES

During the Second World War only one cat was awarded the Dickin Medal, the animal equivalent of the VC. It is usually awarded to dogs and pigeons(!) with a few horses also awarded. The cat was Simon, the mascot of HMS *Amethyst*, and he is buried in the PDSA animal cemetery in Ilford. The award was for fighting off large rats who threatened the sailors' precious food supplies, despite his being injured in attacks on the ship by communist forces. He survived the war, and died on 28 November 1949. Simon's medal was sold at auction in 1993 for £23,467.

Arthur the non-pedigree cat became very famous during the 1960s when he appeared in television advertisements for cat food. He was a large, white British short-haired cat who ate the food out of a tin by dipping in his paw and raising the food to his mouth. Arthur's owner died during this period and he was delivered to a cat breeder in Hutton, later moving to a cattery in Abridge when the breeder, too, died. He appeared in over thirty commercials, each one taking

two to three days to make, and became as well known as any human television celebrity. In true celebrity mode, Arthur appeared in court in a battle over ownership (won by Spillers, the cat food manufacturers), and was front-page news in April 1974 when he was kidnapped – or catnapped. The cattery's owner, Mrs Green, found herself with the busiest telephone line in Britain, dealing with all the sightings. Arthur was eventually found, abandoned, in Dunstable and returned to Essex. The cat food was renamed after him in 1992, sixteen years after his death.

NOT FORGETTING THE HORSES

The 11th Baron Petre (1793–1850) was master of his own pack of foxhounds from which the Essex Union Hunt developed, and was the man responsible for the racecourse at Oxney Green, near Writtle. He is also believed to be the man who acquired Marengo, Napoleon's Arabian Gray horse, after the Battle of Waterloo.

The old Toll Gate Cottage at the foot of the steep Gun Hill, Dedham, had an early twentieth-century sign above the door. This advised carters to rest 'on this steep hill. Dumb beasts pray use with all good will.' Hopefully the carters took the advice.

A blacksmith in Witham (Melvin Baker) appeared in the *Guinness Book of Pet Records* after making a replica horseshoe which was originally created for the biggest horse in the world. The supersize horseshoe measured 14in across. Mr Baker's business was certainly an ancient one, because, according to historians, pack mules were shod on the site 1,000 years ago.

More Quirky Animal Stories

When Elizabeth Balls lived on the green at Havering-atte-bower between 1785 and 1823 she filled her cottage with animals. At one time, as many as 50 goats, 17 chickens, 2 sheep and a cat and a poodle were in residence. This menagerie was a response to being jilted, as she scorned all human company as a result.

The herd of Kashmir goats at Windsor Great Park started as a donation from the Tower family of the Weald Hall Estate in 1828. King George IV had so admired them on a visit that the family arranged for some to be imported as a gift.

Although Dr John Salter of D'Arcy House, Tolleshunt D'Arcy (1864–1932) was a world famous dog judge and Vice President of the Kennel Club, he did not seem that interested in animal rights. While hunting in Russia with the czar and the Grand Duke Nicholas, he shot two brown bears and shipped them (stuffed) back to England to ornament his drawing room. The same treatment was given to four wolves that he shot on a second trip in 1901.

A monologue by Stanley Holloway ('Albert and the Lion') may have been inspired by Wallace, the stuffed lion at Saffron Walden Museum. The lion was originally part of George Wombwell's early travelling zoo, George being based at Duddenhoe End. (It has to be said, however, that other lions around the country have laid claims as this very same inspiration). Was Wallace the same Wombwell lion who was said to have decapitated a female assistant when her long hair tickled the inside of his mouth? Records are unclear – but Wombwell's Menagerie, regardless, continued to tour until 1931 when it was one of only two remaining in the country.

The motorcycling daredevil who became famous in the 1950s for his appearances on the Wall of Death at the Kursaal in Southend-on-Sea, George 'Tornado' Smith, pioneered the use of animals in his act. His lioness, Briton, sat either on the petrol tank or the cross-bar until she grew too big when Smith had to make a sidecar for her.

Up to 165 ferrets at one time have been successfully looked after at the Colchester and District Ferret and Bird of Prey Rescue. The animals are often picked up as strays, mostly by the RSPCA.

Unusual Essex Pets

A pet chinchilla was often seen in the summer of 2008 on the streets of Frinton and Clacton. Its teenage owner took the seven-year old rodent, named Tatiana, for walks on a lead.

A rather larger pet, 5ft long and weighing 7kg, is the iguana which belonged to a Manningtree resident. Named Rocky, he has appeared in *The Guinness Book of Records*.

Zoo Time

Colchester Zoo is the only zoo in Essex since Vange Zoo (Basildon area) closed in 2002. The zoo, opened in 1963, now covers more than 60 acres and costs over £1,000 an hour to run. With over half a million visitors a year to see its 2,500 individuals (545 species), the zoo employs over 250 staff.

The zoo is the first in the UK to breed aardvark babies and the only zoo in the UK to have a group of breeding Gelada Baboons. It also has the largest breeding group of mandrills in the UK.

Flossie the Rhino is the longest resident – since 1970 – and Rajang the Orangutan is the oldest at forty-one. Rarest bird is the Waldrapp Ibis ('critically endangered') and rarest mammal is the Amur Leopard with less than forty left in the wild.

Every adult elephant eats 15kg of nuts, 7kg of bananas, 5kg of carrots, 4kg of apples and three loaves of bread every day, not to mention additional hay, leaves and vitamins. The first baby elephant born at the zoo, Kito, was the first in the world to arrive after just one artificial insemination treatment.

TREES AND FORESTS

Hatfield Forest is Britain's best preserved small hunting forest. This Site of Special Scientific Interest (SSSI), one of seven National Nature Reserves, was created by the Normans for the royal family, and survives relatively unscathed. Its 1,049 acres are home to deer and cattle as well as to woodlands, grassland and fen.

Britain's oldest deciduous tree is an oak in Hatfield Broad Oak. It is reputed to be 800 years old.

Anglo-Saxons laid 40,000 oak trees in about 690 to connect the Essex mainland with Mersea Island. The remains form part of the causeway known as the Strood, liable to flooding at high tide. More recently – between 1950 and 1960 – 100,000 trees were planted around Basildon by the town's council.

Hangman's Woods at Little Thurrock are not what they seem: the name refers to the trees hanging over the marshland.

The timber from Hainault Forest (SSSI) was used to build ships for the Royal Navy in the sixteenth century. The area was deforested from 1851 onwards, but, before that, it was a place offering plenty of employment to the locals. Job titles that do not appear on many passports included verderers (inspectors), foresters (looking after game), reeves (looking after pastures), stewards (supervising other forest staff), regarders (monitoring forest management), woodwards (looking after trees) and Master of the Forest (looking out for poachers, bearing in mind the area was alive with wildcat, hart, hind, hare and boar, plus marten, fox, badger, red deer, doe and buck).

In 1740, 4,970 trees were planted in the grounds of Thorndon Hall, Ingrave, by Lord Petre, all grown in his nurseries from seed imported from America. Names included the Virginia Tulip tree and the Pennsylvania Cherry. Over the following two years, a further 40,000 trees were planted, and he left an astonishing 219,925 plants in his nurseries when he died of smallpox at the age of just twenty-nine in 1742.

A chestnut tree at George Green, Wanstead, dating back to around 1750, was recognised by the High Court as a legal dwelling because the Post Office delivered mail to it from around the world.

A woodcutter from Loughton, Thomas Willingale, was among those who fought to hang on to lopping rights for commoners in Epping Forest because branches thus lopped were 'free' winter forest fuel for many people. He managed to prolong the rights, but not secure them. In 1882, Queen Victoria dedicated the forest for the enjoyment of the public in perpetuity, lopping no longer being lawful. In the twenty-first century, a large proportion of Epping Forest has been designated a Site of Special Scientific Interest. Before the Civil War, it comprised 60,000 acres, now reduced to 6,000, but is home to 80 artificial ponds, 500 rare insects and 50 different types of tree.

A giant willow planted in Boreham in 1835 was felled in 1888 to make cricket bats. Weighing 11 tons, the 101ft tall tree made 1,179 bats.

The yew tree has a reputation as an omen of impending doom. Appropriately, it was chosen by Sarah Chesham, the nineteenth-century poisoner from Ponds Manor, Clavering, as the spot to hide her poisons. Doom indeed, for she was executed in 1851.

A network of wartime trenches were dug by the London Defence Volunteers in Norsey Wood as part of the inner London defence line. The area, some 175 acres, is now famous for its bluebells and is part of the national dormouse monitoring programme. Norsey is another SSSI and a scheduled ancient monument.

The Wild Service Tree, although rare, thrives in Broaks Wood in Sible Hedingham. It looks like a maple tree, but its common name is Chequers, and it used to be grown in pubs brewing their own beer. The berries were used to clear the beer, and there was also an alcoholic beverage named after the tree, called, predictably, the Chequers. This probably explains the number of public houses in existence called The Chequers.

FIG. 32.—A netful of mud with its inhabitants: 1,
Cænis; 2, *Tubifex;* 3, worm, *Nais;* 4, *Tricorythus;* 5,
mud-tubes of midges; 6, nematode worm; 7, snail.

A Few Other Sites of Special Scientific Interest in Essex

Plenty to choose from with 80 per cent of the Essex coastline designated, but Canvey Wick can be singled out because it was the first major brownfield site named as a SSSI, i.e. a protected conservation area, although on the site of a derelict oil terminal beside a giant superstore. The area has a greater biodiversity per square foot than any other site in the UK making it 'Britain's rainforest'. It plays host to such rarities as thirty endangered invertebrates including the weevil-eating wasp and the brown-banded carder-bee, and, for example, over 300 species of moth. Several insects found were so rare they had not been given English names. The Canvey Horticultural Society, incidentally, were very busy back in 1953 importing earthworms from the mainland – to redress the balance as a result of so many disappearing, or dying, in the flooding.

The largest heron colony in Essex is within the 175-acre site at the Gunpowder Mills Museum in Waltham Abbey, an area also occupied by otters and rare orchids. Just a mile away is Cornmill Meadows, the only dragonfly sanctuary in the country that is open to the public.

Although now run by the Essex Wildlife Trust, Hanningfield Reservoir was built in the 1950s to supply water to the growing population of South Essex. It is significant for its population of coot, pochard and tufted duck.

The Great Shellbanks at Foulness Point are made almost entirely of cockleshells from cockle-beds further along the Essex coastline. The area is the largest of its kind in Europe, reshaped constantly by weather and water. Similarly, Bradwell-on-Sea has 'sand' which is actually millions of shells broken down by the waves.

The mudflats around Two Tree Island at Leigh-on-Sea are of international importance due to the large numbers of Brent Geese which arrive in early autumn. Up to 20,000 fly in from Siberia, 2,500 miles away, to feed on the plentiful eel grass.

Planned for 2023 is 'Wildspace' at Rainham Marshes, the biggest new green space to be created in Eastern England for more than 100 years. It will be triple the size of London's Hyde Park and Kensington Gardens combined, amounting to some 1,500 acres.

GREEN FINGERS IN ESSEX

At a time when a tulip bulb could cost as much as a house (the early seventeenth century), an Epping aristocrat, Lionel Cranfield of Copped Hall, seems to have been the first man to grow them in the county. His enterprise did not make his fortune, however, for he moved out of Copped (or Copt) Hall in 1636 for 'reasons of economy'.

The first gardenia in England was cultivated from seed in 1758 in a greenhouse in Woodford Green. Richard Warner acquired the seed in the Cape of Good Hope, and spent four years on its cultivation, with eventual success.

In the eighteenth century, the 80 acres of botanic gardens at Upton House, West Ham (then in Essex), were apparently only rivalled by Kew. At one point, a number of artists were commissioned to record the beauty of the plants, and their paintings were eventually sold to Empress Catherine II of Russia: 2,000 of them for about £2,300.

In the nineteenth century, Charles Darwin used samples of oxlip from Essex in his work, as did Henry Doubleday, the Epping naturalist. The parish of Great Bardfield had 'meadows yellow with oxlips' and the flower appeared on the village coat of arms. It is a nationally scarce plant only growing where Essex, Suffolk and Cambridgeshire meet, but numbers have declined dramatically in the last few decades.

The traditional county flower of Essex is the cowslip (related to the primrose), sometimes known locally as the peggle, or more formally *Primula veris*. Its future may be assured by its use in the wild-flower seed mixes used to landscape motorway cuttings and similar earthworks. Other flowers with Essex links include the Red Poppy and the Essex Rose, not forgetting Tendring sea-lavender which is said to grow nowhere else in the world.

Although George Stacey Gibson (1818–83), author of *Flora of Essex*, identified 1,070 native and naturalised species growing in Essex, the eccentric Ellen Willmott (1858–1934) of Warley Place, Brentwood, is said to have grown 100,000 varieties of plant in her gardens, of which she could remember 36,000. She had 104 gardeners at one point, although this may have included those employed in the gardens of her four overseas properties.

Beth Chatto Gardens at Elmstead Market was created from an overgrown wasteland (from 1960) with a gravel garden filled with drought-loving plants. Famously successful, the gravel garden has never been artificially irrigated; very useful when hose-pipe bans rule.

Barnards Farm Gardens in West Horndon is the home of the National Collection of Malus (Crab apples), but is unusual for more than this reason. The sprawling 17 hectares house more sculptures than the National Gallery, and incorporate a Euro Wood. It also has its own airstrip, cycle shop and a collection of working vintage cars. Such a labour of love has required a lot more than green fingers.

TOP TEN ESSEX (FEATHERED) BIRDS (THE TWITCHERS' GUIDE)

Starling
House sparrow
Blue tit
Collared dove
Black bird
Wood-pigeon
Greenfinch
Great tit
Chaffinch
Robin

However, if Essex had a county bird, writers such as the late Samuel Bensusan feel that it should be the lapwing, or peewit, whose cry reflects the sense of the Essex marshes. There are also five species of owl 'spottable' in Essex – barn, tawny, little, short-eared and long-eared.

BIRD BANTER

Abberton Reservoir, 4 miles north of the River Blackwater, is internationally famous as a wildfowl refuge. It has a water surface area of 1,240 acres and circumference of 12 miles, with 214 different species listed by 1968 including nineteen varieties of waders alone. It is the only place in Britain where the gull-billed tern has been known to nest. Similar numbers of bird varieties have been recorded at Fingringhoe Wick, the flagship of Essex Wildlife Trust on the Colne Estuary, and at Foulness which claims to have been visited by 90 per cent of the country's oystercatchers and a third of the world population of Brent geese.

Skipper's Island at Kirby-le-Soken (Hamford Water Natural Nature Reserve) comprises 233 acres and is home to nightingales, short-eared owls, kestrels, black-headed gulls, Brent geese, curlew, gadwall, godwit, shelduck, oystercatcher and redshank. It is also a haunt for the Fisher's Estuarine moth discovered in 1968, the Roesel's bush cricket and the Essex Skipper butterfly. The area was fictionalised in Arthur Ransome's *Secret Water*, with the island renamed Mastodon Island.

There remain now only remnants of decoy ponds for ducks which were used into the twentieth century at Steeple on the River Blackwater. These were dug in 1713 with the cost of construction paid for in the first winter after 7,364 ducks were caught and sold. Decoy ponds in the county date back to the thirteenth century or even earlier, but the advent of guns signalled their demise. Punt gunners were able to kill many ducks with one shot from the large guns (with up to 900 shot) they used in their punts.

In October 1817, the villages of Stanford Rivers were so plagued by sparrows that the churchwardens offered four pence for every dozen dead ones that were brought to them.

CREEPY CRAWLIES

Hainault Forest has been listed as a 'nationally important invertebrate site.' Some 940 species have been listed, of which 7 were endangered species and a further 79 'nationally scarce'.

The European Scorpion – small, and with weaker venom than its bigger brothers – has been found at Colchester, Harwich – and at Ongar tube station.

The winged antlion, usually found in the USA, was discovered for only the second time in this country at a St Osyth farm in the summer of 2006. The sighting was believed to be attributable to the unexpectedly high temperatures.

The common adder (and lizard) abounds along some stretches of the River Crouch. However, the home of the largest adder population in the UK is said to be Danbury Common, near Chelmsford.

Just one square metre of Thames Estuary mud can hold up to 1,200 worms below the surface, with up to 15,000 snails grazing on the surface.

12

RIVERS AND COAST

WATERY DISASTERS

Copies of the *Essex Review* (1900 and 1928) give accounts of whales 'taken' around the Essex coastline after being stranded. It took eight horses 'with double tackle' to turn such a whale over in 1849 at Grays. This hefty mammal produced 13 tons of blubber and 20 tons of meat, with the process of cutting up and boiling the whale 'occupying seven men for eight days.' Another 'monstrous' whale was killed 'about a dozen' miles from Colchester in about 1677, some 42ft long and 'of bigness proportionable.' This whale had ended up in a narrow creek after heavy winds off the coastline, and attracted 'multitudes' of people 'as thick as to a market or fair.'

Shipwrecks were common during the eighteenth and nineteenth centuries, one of the worst nights being 12 December 1849. This was a night of strong winds and heavy rain, resulting in six vessels going down – five carrying coal from Newcastle to London and another foreign vessel. All the ships were stranded on the Gunfleet Sands, but, thanks to the aid of a passing cutter (HMS *Scout*) most of the crews were rescued and taken to Harwich.

The Gunfleet Sands (running from the Naze to the Colne) were also responsible for the grounding of the *Johann Friedrich*, a 305-ton vessel, in 1850. The 160 passengers (mostly female) were emigrants en route from Bremen to the New World. In spite of the strong winds and hazy conditions, a number of fishing smacks from Wivenhoe and Harwich went to their aid, saving the unexpected cargo.

The loss of ninety-eight passengers and crew was the outcome when the *Deutschland*, carrying emigrants to New York from Germany, struck a sandbank off Harwich in December 1875. The ship had no lifeboat and those boats attempting to aid the ship during a snowstorm capsized in the rough, stormy seas. The level of lives lost led to a lifeboat station at Harwich soon afterwards.

Barking Creek was the site of the sinking of the paddle-steamer *Princess Alice* in September 1878. It was the worst ever shipping disaster at the time, with over 600 of the 900 on board being drowned.

In January 1902, two steam-ships en route from London to India collided in the Thames Estuary; the *Ben Mohr,* carrying 3,000 tons of cement, and the *Banffshire*. The able captains were able to drive their vessels 'hard up' on the muddy shore at Canvey Island (Hole Haven), saving their crews with their actions.

When the Little Ships of Leigh-on-Sea set off for Dunkirk in May 1940 as part of an armada of volunteers to assist the evacuation of British soldiers, they successfully ferried some 1,000 from shore to the waiting large ships at anchor in deep water. The cockle boats *Renown, Leticia, Reliant, Endeavor, Resolute* and *Defender* were on their way home when the *Renown* hit a mine, killing the crew of fishermen on board. A sad end for a heroic crew.

The *Mi Amigo* was the converted cargo boat that housed Radio Caroline in the 1960s, moored off the Frinton shore. During a storm in January 1966 she broke free and crashed on to the coast, but Radio Caroline was back on track after just a few weeks (on a different boat) although outlawed by British and Dutch governments. It was finally towed away in 1968. After being relaunched in 1972, it was finally silenced by another storm in 1980 and the first disc jockeys ever to be saved from the sea were rescued with some difficulty, 13 miles off the Southend coast, by the *Helen Turnbull* lifeboat.

Essex Islands

With more than thirty islands within the county's borders, Essex incorporates more than any other English county. Of these, Mersea is the most easterly inhabited island off the coast of England, Canvey is the fourth most populated and Foulness is the fourth largest.

Osea Island has two claims to fame: in the mid-nineteenth century Frederick Nicholas Charrington of the brewery family sold his shares after seeing a drunk punch his wife during a domestic. Altogether, he raised a million pounds to open a home for inebriates on the island, a secluded self-contained place. However, the locals found it profitable to smuggle drink into the residents or hire boats out to them so they could fetch their own alcohol. Still, he meant well. Later, during the First World War, it became a secret Admiralty base known as HMS *Osea* for constructing and testing coastal motor boats. These boats – with torpedoes – were used successfully in Russia in 1919.

Canvey Island was known in the early twentieth century as Ye Olde Dutch Island, and sometimes as Holland-in-England, thanks to its origins at the hands of Dutch builders, and has been described as a 'unique health resort'. Apart from the landfill site, the only part of Canvey that is above sea level is the man-made sea-wall. A.P. Herbert, the author and politician, was not a fan. As a petty officer based on Southend Pier (during the Second World War) he recommended that the island be sacrificed to 'save London' in time of flooding.

Navigating the Waters

The principal waterways in Essex are the:

Blackwater	Can
Brain	Chelmer
Cam	Ching

Colne (the longest, at 39 miles)	Rom
Crouch	Roman
Ingrebourne	Slade
Lea	Stort
Mardyke	Stour
Pant	Ter
Roach	Wid
Roding	

A ferry service operated between Rainham (The Three Crowns) and Erith in Kent from the twelfth century. Several hundred years later, there were stories that even a Rainham Ferry rock was produced for visitors from London.

Coggeshall boasts the oldest brick bridge in the country, spanning the River Blackwater. It was constructed in about 1220 with small but distinctive bricks made locally, bringing brick-making back to Essex for the first time since the Roman occupation.

The ancient road to Foulness was known as the Broomway, as the route across the sands was originally made by placing broom branches at intervals, a common fifteenth-century method. It could only be used when the tide was out.

The first official direct mails between Harwich and Holland, the Harwich Packets, operated from 1635. The service was still operational until 1832 when the Post Office (as it was then known) switched to using steamships. Harwich is now best known for the ferries which sail for the Hook of Holland, Germany and Scandinavia.

The barges at Burnham and Bradwell were the only ones to deliver goods to London during the plague, resulting in privileged trade status in later years.

The first recorded ferry between Brightlingsea and Point Clear ran in 1699. The service has not run continually, however, though a ferry service was reinstated as recently as 2004. The 1925-built MS *Brightlingsea* ran between Suffolk and Essex for seventy years, and survives as a restored passenger boat.

A steam ferry service replaced sailing and rowing boats between Tilbury and Gravesend in Kent in 1855. Car ferries between the two locations were introduced in 1924, and a catamaran – *Great Expectations* – took over in 1992 to cater for the now reduced demand (the Dartford Tunnel under the Thames from 1963 had obviated the need for a ferry).

The Thames Sailing Barges were once the principal way of transporting goods between London and the east coast ports. There were over 5,000 of them by 1860, but only a few dozen remain. The distinctive brown sails can still be seen at the barge races which take place around the coast in the summer months.

Stackies were Thames barges loaded with straw or hay half-way up the masts which looked like sailing haystacks. The hay was needed to meet the tremendous demand for animal feed and litter in London in the nineteenth century – mainly horses on the street, but also cows kept in barns for individual milk supplies.

The Queen Elizabeth II (or QE2) Bridge, linking Essex and Kent 65 metres above the River Thames, was opened in October 1991 by the queen. It is the longest cable-stayed bridge in Europe – at 2,872 metres including approaches – and was the first fully privatised infrastructure project in the United Kingdom in the twentieth century.

Lighthouses and Lifeboats

Founded by Henry VIII in 1514, Trinity House (whose operational control centre is based at Harwich) looks after the safety of shipping and seafarers, and is responsible for the lighthouse service. The control centre is responsible for remote lighthouse operation up and down the country. Harwich itself had High and Low lighthouses used together in the nineteenth century – when the lights of both were in line, the line indicated a safe shipping channel.

The first telephonic communication between lighthouse and shore was initiated at Frinton in 1893. A cable was laid on the sea bed from the lighthouse on Gunfleet Sands to Frinton Capway.

Lionel Lukin, born at Little Dunmow in May 1742, is credited with the invention of the first unsinkable lifeboat. It was essentially a shell with air-bags around it, and he tested his model on what is known as the Doctor's Pond in the village. It was patented in 1795.

The Essex Lifeboat Association came into being on New Year's Day 1821, the first lifeboat being established at Harwich, closely followed by Brightlingsea.

The coxswain of Southend's first lifeboat, William Bradley, saved twenty-seven lives at sea in the nineteenth century. He lived as the light keeper at the end of Southend Pier for twenty years, and seems to have found it more expedient on occasion to just jump into the sea feet first from the seaweed-clad roof of his home to save an errant swimmer or boater rather than use a boat.

The oldest surviving motorised lifeboat in the world is the *James Stevens No. 14* at Walton on the Naze.

Salty Tales

There are forty-five salt pans listed on the North Essex Coast in the Domesday Book. Most of these were around Tendring, Winstree and Thurstable, giving modern-day names such as Salcott, from the saltcotes where salt was manufactured or stored.

The Blackwater River is renowned for its areas of saltings and mud ooze, and, during the summer, evaporation leaves a large residue of salt behind which is swept up to Maldon on the tide. It is 'trapped' here and boiled to produce crystal salt, an ancient industry dating back to before the Romans. After 2,000 years of salt production in the area, it was Maldon Salt Works that became the only sea salt factory in Britain (in 1894) and it has enjoyed renewed acclaim since television chefs have praised its mild and crumbly crystals.

The production of salt in Essex left a number of red hills, a by-product coloured by the clay pots in which seawater was heated to evaporation point. These hills are actually inland now as a result of land reclamation.

During the days of smuggling on the River Crouch, illicit casks of brandy were attached to heavy blocks of salt which sank beneath the waters. When the salt dissolved, the packages surfaced, ready for the smugglers to retrieve.

The Essex coast is home to a larger area of salt marsh than any other British county.

SOME OFFSHORE SURPRISES

TS *Exmouth* was an old, wooden-walled ex-battleship that had seen service at Balaclava, but was used from 1876 as a training ship for 'poor boys chargeable to Metropolitan parishes and unions.' The ship was moored at Grays, and the '*Exmouth* boys' were trained in sea-going skills. Some famous names who spent teenage years on the *Exmouth* were Eric Morley (the Miss World man) who learnt how to play the French horn, a skill he never lost, and Sydney Chaplin (brother of Charlie) who learned to be a bugler. Another training ship, the *Cornwall*, moored off Purfleet in the nineteenth century, provided a similarly disciplined regime for the education of boys in need of care. Even as recently as 1947–8, a training ship (the TS *Joseph Hertz*, named after the Chief Rabbi of Great Britain) was moored off Grays, this time for Jewish orphans, some of whom came from Belsen.

At the beginning of the twentieth century, smallpox ships were anchored in the River Thames at Long Reach, Purfleet. A few years later, prison ships were being used including the *Royal Edward*, moored off Southend-on-Sea. This particular ship was unlucky enough to be used as target practice by the German commander of a passing zeppelin (May 1915). The incendiary bomb just missed, but the zeppelin was more successful when dropping bombs over Southend.

It seems that the *Richard Montgomery*, an American-built ship on its way to France during the Second World War, ran aground on a sandbank 2 miles off-shore from Southend-on-Sea. It remains there still – loaded with 3,173 tons of ammunition, with regular checks to ensure its safety! It is the only designated dangerous wreck in British waters, with parts visible above the water-line.

The world's largest offshore wind farm is being built off the Essex coast. It will cover a 144-mile stretch from Clacton-on-Sea to Margate in Kent, targeted for completion in 2011 at a cost of £2 billion.

THOUGHTS ON PORTS AND FORTS

The Harwich Redoubt Fort was built in 1808 to defend against a possible Napoleonic invasion. It is 180ft in diameter, with eleven guns, walls 3ft thick, and surrounded by a dry moat. During a siege, 300 troops could be sheltered.

Tilbury Fort and Coalhouse Fort were built to guard the lower reaches of the River Thames where it narrows towards London. Tilbury is the largest example of seventeenth-century military engineering in England, but has never been tested by enemy action. It remained in military hands until 1950. Coalhouse Fort (built in about 1874 on the site of earlier gun batteries) was the result of the threat of invasion from France. A military garrison to deter enemy vessels, its construction was supervised by General Gordon of Khartoum fame. It remains as the best example of a Victorian armoured fortress in the south-east.

Martello Towers were built along the Essex coast as mini-forts, mainly from bricks from Grays, transported via water. Their construction employed 500 men over several years, and a million bricks were needed for each tower. They could each accommodate thirty men, an ammunition store, two 24lb guns, several smaller cannon, and some had metal tanks to store water in case of siege. They were completed in 1812 ready to receive Napoleon and his troops – hence never used. A few survive in a variety of guises.

Brightlingsea – a maritime heritage town – is privileged to be the only Cinque Port in Essex. Now serving a ceremonial role, Cinque Ports originally had to lend all available ships to the king in time of war, in return for financial concessions.

The Port of Tilbury is the largest container port for timber and paper products in the UK. It took four years to build the original dock (1882–6), with the Cruise Terminal constructed in 1930. The terminal was the destination for the first post-war Caribbean migrants on the *Empire Windrush* from Kingston, Jamaica, in 1948. Today, it is used for the docking of around thirty-five cruise ships each year.

BOATING YARNS

Ship-building in Essex has been the mainstay of many coastal towns in the history of the county. Brightlingsea, for instance, provided ships (and men) for Edward III's siege of Calais in 1347 and for Sir Francis Drake's attack on Lisbon in 1589. More recently, 50ft wooden decoy submarines were built at Wivenhoe shipyard during the early part of the Second World War.

Not just ship-building, but repairs too, were important forms of revenue at one time. Drake (and others) put into Harwich with thirty-five ships in 1588 to re-stock after the (unofficial) defeat of the Spanish Armada. Similarly, Admiral Blake brought his fleet to be refitted at Leigh-on-Sea in 1652 in preference to the Kent ports – although no doubt partly influenced by prevailing winds.

The first recorded reward made to a packet boat captain at Harwich was to Captain Robert Stevens. The captain had beaten off a pirate attack, and William III presented him with a gold medal and chain – which, in 1693, was worth an impressive £60.

There is a seventeenth-century crane standing in Harwich which was used when the town was a royal shipyard building men-of-war to fight the French. The crane was initially powered by two donkeys, and later by teams of sailors who had been captured as prisoners-of-war.

The *Mayflower* is thought to have been built at Leigh-on-Sea, or, at least, fitted out there. Harwich also claims its construction, their claim backed up by the Master of the *Mayflower* being one Christopher Jones of Harwich. A large number of Essex people were among the Pilgrim Fathers who set sail for the Americas in 1620, many from Billericay.

When the Marquis of Anglesey wanted a 130-ton cutter built on his return from Waterloo (1820), he went to Wivenhoe to seek out renowned boat-builder (and small time villain) Philip Sarnty. The idea of building one of the first yachts appealed to a smuggler who had built a boat that could outrun the customs officials. Sarnty was in Chelmsford prison at the time, and persuaded Anglesey to secure his release, and that of his brother and brother-in-law, as a condition of agreeing to do the work. The result was the *Pearl*, a renowned vessel that won much praise for Sarnty's handiwork, and which gave rise to yacht racing as a national sport.

Between 1780 and 1938 some 1,600 sailing smacks were built in Essex (the majority at Brightlingsea), mainly to bring fish to market. Scores of deep sea smacks, known as skillingers, were registered at Colchester and represented the largest dredging fleet around British shores. Many of these were built along the banks of the Colne and the Blackwater, and just one remains. The *Pioneer*, built in 1864, languished for years in West Mersea mud, but was sailing again in 2005 following six years of restoration.

Records indicate that the first Essex sailing barge was built in Rettendon in 1791, and the last Thames steel sailing barge at Mistley in about 1928. The first iron vessel to be built on the Colne was the *Silver Star*, a 25-ton schooner, commissioned in 1857 by a wealthy Mr Bruff. Over fifty years later, the last (and largest) warship was launched on the Thames: HMS *Thunderer* was constructed by the Thames Ironworks at Dagenham Dock in 1912.

HMS *Beagle*, used by Charles Darwin for his ground-breaking five-year voyage (1831–6) to the Galápagos and Patagonia, was put to use as a watch vessel moored in the River Roach as part of the Coastguard Service. The oyster fishers from Burnham-on-Crouch petitioned the Navy to have her moved because she was making the river passage difficult, and she was allocated a mud berth. By 1870, she was sold for scrap to local farmers, but it seems that much of the ship remains buried under the saltings off Paglesham. Scientists are hoping to verify the identity of the wreck using ground-penetrating radar and examining microscopic organisms attached to the wreck to see if they originated in waters known to have been visited by Darwin.

Sir Thomas Lipton, the tea and grocery magnate, kept his yacht *Shamrock* at Mersea. He won the Americas Cup in 1930 at his fourth attempt, with a mainly Mersea crew. A few years later, the flagship of the Royal Burnham Yacht Club's Challenge for the Americas Cup (1938) was MV *Kalizma*, an Edwardian yacht owned by the Burtons (Richard and Liz) in their heyday.

13

ON THIS DAY

1 January 1915   Train crash at Ilford killed ten people, with a
                 further eighty injured.

2 January 1999   Essex cricketer Nasser Hussain played for England
                 in Sydney, Australia.

3 January 1912   Lawrence Oates of Gestingthorpe was chosen for
                 Scott's polar expedition.

4 January 1949   Basildon designated a New Town.

5 January 1941   Amy Johnson crashed and died off the coast near
                 Shoeburyness.

6 January 1899   A boiler explosion at Hewett's Engineering,
                 Barking, killed ten men, injuring many others.

7 January 1434   Messing-born Richard Baynard, lawyer and
                 speaker of the House of Commons, died.

8 January 1856   Charles Spurgeon, Kelvedon's preacher/writer,
                 married convert Susannah Thompson.

9 January 1999   Jim Peters, marathon runner, died at Westcliff-on-
                 Sea.

10 January 1798 Baron Braybrooke (born Richard Neville) became
                 Lord Lieutenant of Essex.

11 January 1406 Death of former Archbishop of Canterbury Robert
                 Walden of Walden (later Saffron Walden).

12 January 1905 Death of James Mason, Irish-born chess master, at
                 Rochford.

13 January 1951 Dorothea Bate, renowned palaeontologist, died at
                 Westcliff-on-Sea.

14 January 1814 Frost Fair held on the frozen River Thames.

15 January 1436 Robert Fitzhugh, Bishop of London, died
                 (St Osyth).

16 January 1959	Sultry singer Sade, who grew up in Clacton, was born.
17 January 1800	Chelmsford Church collapsed when grave diggers dug too close to a supporting pillar.
18 January 1881	Twenty-four hour blizzard swept away part of Southend Pier.
19 January 1966	*Mi Amigo* (housing Radio Caroline) lost anchorage and ran aground at Holland-on-Sea.
20 January 1885	Inspector Simmons murdered near Romford.
21 January 2007	Ronnie O'Sullivan (Essex snooker player) won the final of the Masters at Wembley.
22 January 1920	Birth of Alf Ramsey (Dagenham), England's football manager during World Cup 1966.
23 January 1909	Marconi's wireless telegraph (Chelmsford-based) saved 1,500 on the sinking RMS *Republic*.
24 January 1965	Death of Winston Churchill, once MP for Wanstead and Woodford.
25 January 1533	Anne Boleyn (of Rochford Hall, Rochford) married Henry VIII.
26 January 1865	Ferdinand Kohl's was the last public execution in Essex at Chelmsford (for murder).
27 January 2007	Paul Channon, a Southend Conservative MP for nearly forty years, died at Brentwood.
28 January 1834	The Revd Sabine Baring-Gould born, prolific author during his Mersea years.
29 January 1939	Germaine Greer, Essex resident, born.
30 January 1847	Easton Lodge – the Great Dunmow mansion – destroyed by fire.
31 January 1953	Floods meant evacuation of 10,000 Canvey Island residents, with fifty-eight fatalities.
1 February 1802	Explosion at Waltham Abbey powder mills killed nine people.

2 February 1371	Richard Baynard, House of Commons speaker, born at Messing.
3 February 1742	Dr James Bradley of Wanstead appointed Astronomer Royal.
4 February 1975	Ivy Davis found murdered in Westcliff-on-Sea (with no arrest until 2006).
5 February 1381	Henry IV married Mary Bohun at Rochford Hall, Rochford.
6 February 1954	Clacton's Vivian Woodward (legendary footballer and tennis player) died.
7 February 1879	Coldest night in Essex records with -21°C at Aveley.
8 February 1944	The American Silver Streaks arrived at Stansted to launch bombing raids on German-occupied Europe.
9 February 2003	First 'Stop Stansted Expansion' conference held at Stansted Hilton.
10 February 1912	Joseph Lister from Upton, innovator of antiseptic surgery, died.
11 February 1840	First Chief Constable of Essex appointed – Captain John McHardy, a Scotsman.
12 February 1935	The de Bois sisters committed suicide by jumping out of a private aeroplane over Upminster.
13 February 1922	George Pearce killed himself after a bungling attempt to murder Alice Vincent in Southend-on-Sea.
14 February 1996	Eva Hart, *Titanic* survivor from Chadwell Heath, died.
15 February 1833	Benjamin Disraeli wrote to his sister from Southend-on-Sea referring to its 'softer clime' and 'sunnier skies.'
16 February 1736	Massive storm and flooding at Canvey and Foulness resulted in death of all livestock (but not humans).

17 February 1939	John Leyton ('Johnny, Remember Me', etc.) born at Frinton-on-Sea.
18 February 2006	Ryanair launched services to Balaton (Hungary) and Lamezia (Italy) from Stansted.
19 February 1928	First speedway race in England took place behind the King's Oak, Loughton.
20 February 1999	Sarah Kane, controversial Ilford-born playwright, died in London.
21 February 1915	The first air-raid in Essex had a devastating effect in Colchester.
22 February 1856	The stone staircase at Shire Hall, Chelmsford, collapsed when 200 people were fighting their way in to see five poachers being tried for murder.
23 February 1633	Samuel Pepys, twice MP for Harwich, born.
24 February 1993	Barking golden boy Bobby Moore died.
25 February 1601	The Earl of Essex beheaded for treason.
26 February1885	An explosion at Shoebury Barracks resulted in seven fatalities and many injuries.
27 February1601	(St) Anne Line of Dunmow was the last woman to be hanged in England for harbouring priests.
28 February 1745	Captain Samuel Bonham, slave trader from Orsett, died.
29 February 1976	Essex-based Arthur, the Kattomeat cat, died.
1 March 1721	Edward Bright, who became England's heaviest man, was born at Maldon.
2 March 1887	William Shaen, radical lawyer, political reformer and humanitarian (from Hatfield Peverel) died in London.
3 March 1952	Dunmow station was closed to passengers.
4 March 1681	William Penn (raised Wanstead, schooled Chigwell) obtained the charter for Pennsylvania.

5 March 1992	Ilford-born poet Ruth Pitter was buried.
6 March 1944	The first 'action' from the new Stansted Airport when thirty-seven B-26s took off to raid Bernay St Martin airfield.
7 March 1918	Two wartime planes collided above Shotgate (near Wickford) killing the pilots.
8 March 1978	Essex boy Douglas Adams heard the first episode of his *Hitchhiker's Guide to the Galaxy* broadcast on Radio Four.
9 March 1982	The Rt. Hon. Lord Butler of Saffron Walden died.
10 March 1567	Following a collision during a football match in Hatfield Broad Oak, Henry Ingold of White Roding died.
11 March 1952	Author Douglas Adams – later associated with Brentwood – was born.
12 March 1785	Robert Wright was the first to be executed at the new county gaol at Chelmsford (for murder).
13 March 1897	Author Joseph Conrad (*Heart of Darkness*, etc) and his wife moved to Billet Lane in Stanford-le-Hope.

14 March 1903	Official opening of Ilford electric tramways.
15 March 1991	New terminal at Stansted Airport opened by the queen.

16 March 1555   Thomas Higbed burned at the stake at Horndon-on-the-Hill for refusing to embrace Catholicism.

17 March 1880   Birth and death of Captain Lawrence Oates of
and 1912   Gestingthorpe, Antarctic explorer.

18 March 2005   Mersea Island Brewery opened.

19 March 1804   Execution of Elizabeth Langham (for murdering her baby), the only woman hanged at Moulsham in Chelmsford.

20 March 1980   Radio Caroline pirate ship sank 13 miles off Southend coast in heavy seas: the four DJs on board were safely rescued.

21 March 1871   The Revd Sabine Baring-Gould arrived at St Edmunds, East Mersea, where he produced many books set in Essex (at least one, *Mehalah*, still in print).

22 March 1899   Cyril Caunter, aviation historian and author, born in Ilford.

23 March 1971   Basil Dearden, Hollywood film director born in Westcliff-on-Sea, was killed in an accident on the M4.

24 March 1820	Thomas Fairhead from Rochford and Henry Gilliott from Prittlewell were the last men to be hanged at Moulsham for stealing sheep.
25 March 1891	The Salvation Army put down a deposit to purchase 800 acres of farmland at Hadleigh (for £12,000) to give work and training to the East London destitute.
26 March 1555	William Hunter of Brentwood (aged nineteen) was burned at the stake for his Catholic stance.
27 March 2002	Dagenham-born Dudley Moore died.
28 March 1843	Eastern Counties Railway completed a rail link between London and Colchester.
29 March 1964	Radio Caroline started broadcasting off Frinton on board *Mi Amigo*.
30 March 1964	Battle between mods and rockers in Clacton-on-Sea.
31 March 1926	John Fowles, author of *The French Lieutenant's Woman*, born in Leigh-on-Sea.
1 April 1964	The first traffic wardens appeared in Essex.
2 April 1889	The first official meeting of Essex County Council was held in the Shire Hall, Chelmsford.
3 April 1974	Dagenham's Alf Ramsey had his last football match as England manager (in Portugal).
4 April 1820	A bare-knuckle battle took place at Rettendon Common watched by 7,000 people but finished in just eight and a half minutes in a knock-out.
5 April 1827	Joseph Lister (inventor of antiseptic techniques in surgery) born in Upton.
6 April 1936	The 'Greatest Flying Flea Rally Ever' held at Canute Air Park, Ashingdon.
7 April 1739	Hempstead highwayman Dick Turpin executed.
8 April 1817	Eleven prisoners escaped from the old County Gaol in Moulsham, Chelmsford (through the sewers).

9 April 1996   Ilford-born actress Greer Garson buried in Dallas.

10 April 2002   Memorial service held for Mary Whitehouse, Essex
                    morality campaigner.

11 April 1840   First constables of the new county police force
                    appeared in Chelmsford.

12 April 1941   Bobby Moore, football legend, born in Barking.

13 April 1854   Barking station opened.

14 April 1912   While it was sinking, the band on *Titanic* played
                    'Nearer My God to Thee' by Sarah Adams (written
                    in Loughton in 1840).

15 April 1893   Sergeant Adam Eves was murdered by grain thieves
                    at Purleigh.

16 April 1915   Over twenty bombs were dropped on Maldon
                    during a zeppelin raid.

17 April 1886   Tilbury Dock opened.

18 April 1807   A ferry capsized at Harwich Port, with the loss of
                    sixty lives (mostly soldiers).

19 April 1935   Hollywood film star and Dagenham boy Dudley
                    Moore was born in London.

20 April 1950   Warwick Deeping, popular 1940s author born in
                    Southend-on-Sea, died aged 73.

21 April 1997   Essex snooker player Ronnie O'Sullivan achieved
                    the fastest recorded maximum break at 5 minutes
                    20 seconds during the world championships.

22 April 1884   An earthquake struck Colchester, resulting in a
                    couple of deaths and substantial devastation.

23 April 1796   Barges started using the new canal between
                    Heybridge and Chelmsford.

24 April 1871   Michael Campbell was the first to be executed out
                    of the public gaze at Springfield Gaol, Chelmsford.

25 April 1946   Digby Fairweather, jazz musician, was born at
                    Rochford.

26 April 1607	Christopher Newport, from Harwich, landed in Virginia, the new world.
27 April 1899	'Mrs Dougal' moved with her bigamous husband to Clavering (Moat Farm), the site of her eventual murder.
28 April 1854	Charles Spurgeon, Kelvedon's Prince of Preachers, accepted a pastorate in London at the age of nineteen.
29 April 1990	Ilford's Nigel Benn became the WBO Middleweight Boxing Champion.
30 April 1940	German planes crashed at Clacton-on-Sea, killing the first British civilians of the war.
1 May 1964	Stansted Airport became, officially, 'London Stansted'.
2 May 1283	A charter was granted to John de la Mare by King Edward I, allowing a market to be held at Bradwell-on-Sea on Mondays.
3 May 1967	Hungarian-born chess master Stefan Fazekas died at Buckhurst Hill.
4 May 1737	Dick Turpin shot and killed a gamekeeper in Epping Forest.
5 May 1917	Copped Hall, Epping, once owned by Queen Elizabeth I, destroyed by fire.
6 May 1882	Queen Victoria visited High Beach to declare Epping Forest open to the public.
7 May 1589	Andrew Battell, traveller from Leigh-on-Sea, set out across the Atlantic.
8 May 2001	The first ever Agatha Christie Theatre Festival started its run at the Palace Theatre, Westcliff-on-Sea, featuring all twenty-five plays.
9 May 1930	Joan 'Carry On' Sims born at Station House, Laindon.
10 May 1915	Some 150 bombs dropped in attacks on south-east Essex.

11 May 2007	Orsett Hall destroyed by fire hours after a school prom.
12 May 1206	The earliest record of a 'public' school in Colchester.
13 May 1767	Hester Woodley, slave, died at Little Parndon.
14 May 1607	Captain Christopher Newport from Harwich lays the foundations for Jamestown.
15 May 1948	Australian cricketers (vs. Essex) made a record-breaking 721 runs at Southend.
16 May 1829	Bill passed to construct Southend Pier.
17 May 1891	The first thirty workers from East London arrived at General Booth's Home Farm Colony, Hadleigh.
18 May 1742	Lionel Lukin, inventor of the first unsinkable lifeboat, born at Dunmow.
19 May 1906	A meeting at The Blue Boar, Southend-on-Sea, resulted in the launch of Southend United Football Club.
20 May 1904	Margery Allingham, Essex-based crime writer, born.
21 May 1958	The last cattle sale took place at Romford Market after 700 years.
22 May 2001	Actor Jack Watling died at Chelmsford.
23 May 1887	Josephine Collins born, a music hall artiste who lived and died in Epping.
24 May 1888	Romford's cottage hospital opened.
25 May 1832	The owner of Hylands House, Chelmsford, was awarded a medal by the Horticultural Society for his exhibits of forced apricots, raspberries and melons.
26 May 1703	Samuel Pepys, former MP for Harwich, died.
27 May 1974	Denise Van Outen was born in Basildon.

28 May 1877	Warwick Deeping, author, born in Southend-on-Sea.
29 May 1712	Dr Thomas Dimsdale, who 'saved' Catherine the Great from smallpox, born at Theydon Garnon.
30 May 1381	Essex (and Kent) peasants drove out tax collectors at Brentwood.
31 May 1991	The new Brentwood Cathedral was dedicated by Cardinal Hume.
1 June 1889	The first person in Essex to borrow a library book was Alexander Glenny at Barking.
2 June 1797	The Chelmer and Blackwater Canal opened officially.
3 June 1609	Mary Ellis died, described on her gravestone as a '119-year-old virgin from Leigh-on-Sea.'
4 June 1238	Joan, Queen of Scots, died at Havering.
5 June 1813	Murder of Martha Stevens at Woodford (by burglar William Cornwell).
6 June 1945	The double murder of Mr and Mrs Lucas at Leigh-on-Sea (by John Young from Ilford, after an argument over money).
7 June 1329	Death of Robert the Bruce, reputedly born in Writtle.
8 June 1843	Hockley Spa opened to the public.
9 June 1901	Birth at South Woodford of John Skeaping, sculptor, and husband of the more famous Barbara Hepworth.
10 June 1555	Thomas Hawkes of Coggeshall burnt at the stake for his Protestant beliefs.
11 June 1381	20,000 peasants from Essex and Kent set out for London to protest reincreased taxes.
12 June 1912	HMS *Thunderer* completed at Thames Ironworks, Dagenham, the last and largest warship constructed on the Thames.

13 June 1648   The Siege of Colchester (during the Civil War).

14 June 1937   Runwell ('Mental') Asylum was the last such institution to open in Essex (near Wickford).

15 June 1846   The Eastern Union Railway Company opened the Colchester–Ipswich line.

16 June 2007   'The Wedding of the Year' took place between Essex residents Rod Stewart and Penny Lancaster.

17 June 1909   Frederick Page established the first aeronautical engineering company in Britain at Creekmouth, Barking.

18 June 1951   Tenants moved into the first houses in Basildon New Town.

19 June 1834   Renowned preacher and author Charles Spurgeon born at Kelvedon.

20 June 1839   The railway from Mile End (East London) through Ilford to Romford was opened.

21 June 1936   Anti-Air-War memorial unveiled next to the Woodford home of Sylvia Pankhurst.

22 June 1920   St Peter-on-the-Wall at Bradwell-on-Sea was re-consecrated.

23 June 1683   Wanstead's William Penn signed a treaty with the Lenni Lenape tribe in Philadelphia in a bid to ensure peace with 'his' colony in Pennsylvania.

24 June 1897   Freak hailstorm hit Ingatestone, with stones up to 6 inches in diameter killing animals and damaging property.

25 June 1737   Proclamation issued offering £200 reward for capture of Hempstead's Dick Turpin.

26 June 1955   Mervyn Day, the youngest goalkeeper to appear in a FA Cup Final, born in Chelmsford.

27 June 1843   The opening of the Infant Orphan Asylum at Wanstead.

28 June 1381	The Battle of Billericay, the final stand of the Peasants' Revolt.
29 June 1660	King Charles II dined at Copped Hall (then Copt Hall), Epping.
30 June 1717	Three women did public penance in Rettendon Church for adultery and fornication.
1 July 1998	Essex Air Ambulance was launched from the grounds of New Hall School, Chelmsford.
2 July 1550	The Spanish Ambassador sent Jehan Duboys (or Dubois) from Maldon quay to 'rescue' Princess Mary from Protestant rule.
3 July 1846	The body of murdered PC George Clark, aged twenty, was discovered at Dagenham, his killer never caught.
4 July 1912	England's football team beat Denmark 4–2 at the Stockholm Olympics, captained by Vivian Woodward from Clacton-on-Sea.
5 July 1900	Lifeboat *James Stephens No. 14* arrived in Walton on the Naze. It is the town's oldest surviving lifeboat and was restored in 1998.
6 July 1381	Richard II moved to Writtle following the Peasants' Revolt, rendering it the temporary seat of Government.
7 July 1607	Death of the infamous Lady Penelope Rich of Great Leighs and Rochford.
8 July 1754	Stagecoach services initiated between Chelmsford and London (five hours each way).
9 July 1809	Sarah Chesham born at Clavering, destined to become murderess 'Sally Arsenic'.
10 July 1899	Incorporation of Corringham Light Railway.
11 July 1888	Snow fell in Romford, Stock, etc. in the 'year with no summer'.
12 July 1947	Birth of Wilko Johnson (Canvey Island) ex-member of Dr Feelgood.

13 July 1785	General James Oglethorpe, founder of Georgia (USA), died at Cranham (Upminster).
14 July 1942	Work began on Stansted Airport.
15 July 1932	The seaxes (swords) on the Essex coat of arms were granted by the College of Arms.
16 July 1837	John Clare, poet, was admitted to Dr Allen's private lunatic asylum at Fairmead House, High Beach, Epping.
17 July 1648	The Battle of Boxted Heath (Colchester) during the Civil War.
18 July 1871	Clacton Pier opened.

19 July 1821	The biggest street party in Essex, attended by 1,500 people, took place in Chelmsford High Street to celebrate the coronation of King George IV.
20 July 1937	Guglielmo Marconi, Chelmsford radio pioneer, died, and every wireless station in the world observed two minutes' silence.
21 July 1840	Three police constables dismissed at Brentwood for being drunk on duty.
22 July 1904	Death of Chelmsford's Wilson Barrett, the most famous stage actor in England.

23 July 1943	The Rayleigh Bath Chair Murder, when Eric Brown 'blew up' his father.
24 July 1830	Composer and organist Arthur Henry Brown born at Brentwood.
25 July 1829	The first foundation stone laid for Southend Pier.
26 July 1806	Alexander McDonald of the Cameron Highlanders was murdered near Little Clacton, with no-one found guilty.
27 July 1916	Captain Charles Fryatt (from Dovercourt), Master of SS *Brussels*, was shot in Brussels for ramming a German U-boat.
28 July 1904	Start of Colchester's tram system.
29 July 1566	Agnes Waterhouse from Hatfield Peverel executed for witchcraft at Chelmsford, the first trial under new Elizabethan law.
30 July 1966	England wins football's World Cup thanks to an Essex captain (Bobby Moore), Essex manager (Alf Ramsey) and an Essex player (Geoff Hurst).
31 July 1932	Jeremy Lloyd, actor and screenwriter (*'Allo 'Allo*, etc) born at Danbury.
1 August 1883	First balloon crossing across the North Sea took place between Maldon and Flushing.
2 August 1100	King William II of England died in a hunting 'accident', reputedly at the hands of Walter Tyrrell of Langham.
3 August 1863	Last swimming ordeal of a presumed witch in Essex, resulting in the death of a disabled seventy-six-year-old man from Sible Hedingham.
4 August 1588	Sir Francis Drake put into Harwich with thirty-five ships to restock after the unofficial defeat of the Spanish Armada.
5 August 1914	First shot of the First World War fired by HMS *Lance* off Harwich, destroying a German mine-layer.

6 August 1804	Thomas Twining, son of the tea merchant, died at Colchester.
7 August 1917	Edwin Dunning, DSC (from Bradfield, Manningtree), was killed while landing an aeroplane on the deck of a man-of-war.
8 August 1952	Laurel and Hardy were guests of honour at a Palace Hotel function in Southend-on-Sea during their only visit to Essex.
9 August 1588	Queen Elizabeth I gave her famous speech to 12,000 troops at Tilbury.
10 August 1764	Launch of the *Chelmsford Chronicle*.
11 August 1746	Some 268 Jacobite prisoners were landed at Tilbury Fort.
12 August 1647	Purported death of Matthew Hopkins, notorious Essex Witchfinder General.
13 August 1900	The Nathan sisters from Loughton (missionaries) were killed in the Boxer Rising in China.
14 August 1917	Cardew (originally Douglas) Robinson, oddball comedian, born at Goodmayes (Ilford).
15 August 1888	George Sargent from Copford was hanged at Chelmsford for the murder of his estranged wife.
16 August 1893	John Davis executed at Chelmsford for the murder of Sergeant Adam Eves at Purleigh.
17 August 1603	Lady Penelope Rich (wife of Lord Rich of Rochford) granted a noble rank giving her precedence at court over every baroness.
18 August 1909	First – and last – open day at the short-lived Royal Aeronautical Society's flying ground at Dagenham.
19 August 1858	Birth of Ellen Willmott, destined to become the famous, if eccentric, landowner (and gardener) of Warley Place, near Brentwood.
20 August 1944	USS *Richard Montgomery* blown onto the sandbanks off Southend-on-Sea.

21 August 1848	Sarah Adams, writer of hymns and poetry, buried at Harlow, her birthplace.
22 August 1856	Loughton's first railway station opened.
23 August 1906	The Honeypot Lane Murders – a married couple killed by two young brothers in an argument over water, near Basildon.
24 August 1934	Amy Johnson's first flight from Stapleford Tawney Airport, known as Essex Airport.
25 August 1561	Queen Elizabeth I arrived at the manor of Hallingbury Place, Great Hallingbury, on her 'progress'.
26 August 1755	The Lord Mayor of London was in Leigh-on-Sea for the placing of the Crowstone to mark the limits of the City of London's jurisdiction in the Thames.
27 August 1888	Joseph Simmons, famed balloonist, crashed at Ulting.
28 August 1648	Royalist commanders were shot at Colchester Castle during the siege of Colchester.
29 August 1918	Gladys Mills, better known as pianist 'Mrs Mills', was born at Newham, then part of Essex.
30 August 2006	The *Duchess M* ferry out of Tilbury was reported as carrying 50 per cent more people than the permitted sixty, and was subsequently fined £9,000.
31 August 1892	Nunn's Bridge – made by local blacksmith Dick Nunn – opened at Coggeshall over the River Blackwater.
1 September 1905	The Cromer Express disaster at Witham: ten killed and dozens injured.
2 September 1850	Sarah Chesham of Clavering arrested for the murder of her husband.
3 September 1878	The sinking of the *Princess Alice* paddle steamer at Barking Creek, the worst ever shipping disaster (then) with six hundred drowned, two-thirds of those on board.

4 September 1838	George Rush from Elsenham Hall (near Stansted) was the first Essex man to take to the skies – from Vauxhall Gardens, London, in a balloon.
5 September 1938	The largest (then) cinema in Essex, the State, opened at Grays.
6 September 1939	The Battle of Barking Creek, a 'friendly fire' incident.
7 September 1940	A German bomber was brought down at Little Burstead, with two airmen killed and one taken prisoner.
8 September 1823	Sarah Adams, the Harlow poet, broke the female record in her speedy ascent of Ben Lomond.
9 September 1962	The end of steam trains on the Great Eastern Railway.
10 September 1791	Sarah Lee (early naturalist, traveller and author) born Colchester.
11 September 1644	Francis Quarles, 'The Essex Quill', died intestate.
12 September 2001	Russell Brand (from Grays) sacked by MTV after going to work dressed as Osama Bin Laden.
13 September 1983	James Bourne, of Busted and Son of Dork, born at Rochford.
14 September 1820	Essex and Colchester Hospital opened.
15 September 2006	Ilford-born Raymond Baxter, long-serving television presenter, died.
16 September 2007	Essex girl Helen Mirren won an Emmy for *Prime Suspect*.
17 September 1717	The first English-born son of the Dutch royal family, William Henry van Nassan van Zuylestein, born at St Osyth Priory.
18 September 1935	The first municipal airport in Essex opened at Rochford.
19 September 1905	The death of Dr Barnardo, founder of the Barkingside institution.

20 September 1975	Dagenham's Dudley Moore married Hollywood's Tuesday Weld.
21 September 1940	A parachute mine destroyed the pub and church at Little Horkesley.
22 September 2003	Boxer Frank Bruno taken from Brentwood to Goodmayes Hospital, where he was diagnosed with bi-polar disorder.
23 September 2006	Historic Bragg's Mill, Ashdon, reopened after restoration.
24 September 1647	Thaxted Church the site of a fight between parishioners over Lady Maynard's controversial choice of vicar.
25 September 2004	Danny Crates from Heybridge won gold in the 800metres at the Athens Paralympic Games.
26 September 1826	Matthew Sherring, destined to become a renowned missionary in India, born at Halstead.
27 September 1927	The murder of PC George Gutteridge at Stapleford Abbots, despicably shot in both eyes. (His murderers were brought to swift justice and executed.)
28 September 1979	Annika Reeder born in Harlow; the first British gymnast to compete in two Olympics (1996 and 2000).
29 September 1979	First Essex Trophy competition (for change ringers) took place at St Mary's, Southend-on-Sea.
30 September 1308	Elizabeth de Clare, Edward I's granddaughter and Great Bardfield resident, married at Waltham Abbey – went on to found Clare College, Cambridge.
1 October 1934	Ellen Willmott, prize-winning gardener of Warley Place, was buried at Brentwood Cathedral.
2 October 1851	The foundation stone was laid for Essex County Lunatic Asylum, Brentwood.
3 October 1399	Lady Eleanor de Bohun (Thomas of Woodstock's wife) died at Barking Abbey.

4 October 1930	The first practice meeting of the Dagenham Girl Pipers took place.
5 October 1984	Essex police and customs seized the (then) biggest cannabis haul recovered in Britain in a single raid – from a schooner moored at North Fambridge on the River Crouch.
6 October 1900	Stan Morris Nichols (leading 1930s cricketer) born at Stondon Massey.
7 October	St Osyth's Day.
8 October 2000	Death of prolific romantic novelist Sheila Holland, born in Dagenham.
9 October 2005	Severe fire at Southend Pier head.
10 October 2004	The Epping Ongar railway line reopened after ten years thanks to volunteers.
11 October	The Old English Feast Day of seventh-century St Aethelburg of Barking (Abbey).
12 October 1967	Ford's Dunton plant (near Basildon) opened by Harold Wilson.
13 October 1845	Penal reformer Elizabeth Fry died; her remains subsequently removed to the Society of Friends Graveyard in Barking.
14 October 1644	William Penn (founder of Pennsylvania) born – baptised Barking, educated Chigwell.
15 October 1960	The foundation stone was laid for St Martin's Church in central Basildon.
16 October 1987	An unpredicted hurricane did untold damage in Essex.
17 October 1998	Joan (*Miss Marple*) Hickson died, long-term Wivenhoe resident.
18 October 1016	Battle of Assandune took place between Cnut and Edmund (probably at Ashingdon in South Essex, though some suggest Ashdon in North Essex).

19 October 1778 — King George III and Queen Charlotte entertained by Lord Petre at Thorndon Hall, Warley, the first Roman Catholic peer to entertain a monarch.

20 October 1938 — Blonde songstress Kathy Kirby born in Ilford.

21 October 1949 — A headless torso was found on Dengie Flats, but, thanks to the presence of hands – and fingerprints – was identified, and his murderer traced.

22 October 1822 — First brick of Springfield Prison, Chelmsford, laid.

23 October 1548 — Lord Richard Rich (owner of 100 Essex homes) became Lord Chancellor. He was voted most evil sixteenth-century Brit in a BBC *History Magazine* 2006 poll.

24 October 1987 — Heavyweight Essex boxer Frank Bruno knocked out Joe Bugner.

25 October 1850 — The *Johann Friedrich* ran aground on Gunfleet Sands, but the 160 people emigrating to South Carolina from Bremen (mostly female) were saved.

26 October 664 — Bishop Cedd died, ten years after establishing Bradwell-on-Sea mission.

27 October 1974 — The Day family from Aveley 'lost' three hours following an encounter with a UFO.

28 October 1704 — John Locke, renowned philosopher, died at High Laver.

29 October 1662 — William Pynchon – from Springfield, Chelmsford – died having established Springfield, Massachusetts.

30 October 1991 — The queen opened the QE2 Bridge linking Essex to Kent across the Thames.

31 October 1849	Chief Constable William Campling of Saffron Walden was shot. He died nine days later, the crime unsolved.
1 November 1856	William Champ from Maldon appointed the first Premier of Tasmania.
2 November 1941	Brian Poole (of the Tremeloes) born in Barking.
3 November 1994	Ronald Taylor of Barkingside made legal history when he (in addition to ten years in prison) was ordered to forfeit his £15 million profit from cannabis smuggling.
4 November 1914	The last, and oldest, man to be hanged in Essex died at Chelmsford after murdering his wife – Charles Frembd, aged 71.
5 November 1605	Lord Monteagle of Great Hallingbury had been tipped off about the plot to blow up parliament and managed to save the day.
6 November 1871	Henry Hall, a bell-ringer at St Margaret's in Barking, caught his boot in one of the ropes and was killed when he landed on his head.
7 November 1897	Poet Ruth Pitter was born in Ilford.
8 November 1963	The first oast-house theatre in the world was opened by the Rainham Theatrical Society.
9 November 1805	Captain Eliab Harvey (from Chigwell) promoted to Rear Admiral at Trafalgar.
10 November 1750	Edward Bright, renowned fat man from Maldon, died.
11 November 1620	Many Billericay emigrants were among those who landed in the New World on the *Mayflower.*
12 November 1842	Lord John Rayleigh, physicist, died at Witham.
13 November 1969	The first live British quintuplets born in the twentieth century came into the world courtesy of Rayleigh mother Irene Hanson.
14 November	St Erkenwald's Day.

15 November 655   Death of the King of East Anglia, Æthelhere.

16 November 1957   The longest peal ever rung on six bells lasted
                    9 hours 35 minutes at Stisted.

17 November 1890   Decree nisi granted for the notorious Essex-born
                    adulteress, Kitty O'Shea, leaving her free to marry
                    her lover, Charles Stewart Parnell, 'King of Ireland'.

18 November 1963   Dartford Tunnel opened linking Essex to Kent
                    under the Thames.

19 November 1857   The first penny newspaper in Essex, the *Halstead
                    Gazette*, was founded.

20 November   St Edmund's Day.

21 November 1748   John Wesley made first of several visits to Leigh-on-
                    Sea to spread the Methodist message.

22 November 1873   Ramsden Bellhouse windmill blown down.

23 November 2001   Mary Whitehouse, morality campaigner, died in
                    Colchester.

24 November 1990   Dodie Smith, whose written output included *101
                    Dalmatians*, died at her Finchingfield home.

25 November 1974   Basildon railway station opened.

26 November 1862   The last British heavyweight championship to
                    be fought without gloves took place at Fobbing
                    between Jem Mace and Tom King, who won after
                    twenty rounds.

27 November 1703   Henry Winstanley, the inventor from Saffron
                    Walden, died during a coastal storm in the South of
                    England.

28 November 2007   Death of Tony Holland, *Eastenders* creator/
                    scriptwriter from Shoeburyness.

29 November 1897   'Black Monday' featured severe flooding in many
                    parts of Essex.

30 November 1719   Thomas Wood, the dieting miller from Billericay,
                    was born.

1 December 1539   John Beche, Abbot of St John's, Colchester, hanged for dissent.

2 December 1775   Inquest held on Anne Reynolds, eighteen months old from Chipping Ongar, killed in her bed by a pig.

3 December 1923   England cricketer Trevor Bailey born at Westcliff-on-Sea.

4 December 1903   Composer Vaughan Williams made first of several visits to Ingrave collecting 'lost' folk songs.

5 December 1758   Sir Eliab Harvey, the Trafalgar commander, born at Chigwell.

6 December 1875   The *Deutschland* struck a sandbank off Harwich en route to New York with the loss of ninety-eight lives.

7 December 1993   A 250-year-old chestnut tree in Wanstead was chopped down despite violent protests.

8 December 1961   Essex suffragette Ethel Haslam died in Chadwell Heath Hospital.

9 December 1933   The Odeon, Whalebone Lane, Romford opened complete with open-air swimming pool at the rear.

10 December 1827   James Winter was the first man hanged at Springfield Prison, Chelmsford.

11 December 1922   Edith Thompson of Ilford found guilty of her husband's murder and sentenced to death.

12 December 1977   Dean Macey, champion decathlete, born on Canvey Island.

13 December 1902   Death of Henry Doubleday, famous horticulturalist of Coggeshall.

14 December 1379   Alice Perrers (Upminster-based mistress of Edward III) had her sentence of banishment revoked.

15 December 1673   Colchester-born Margaret Lucas died, the most famous authoress of her day.

16 December 1860	Death of Cunning Murrell at Hadleigh, notorious male witch.
17 December 1825	The Chelmsford and Maldon bank of Messrs Crickitt, Russell & Co failed suddenly.
18 December 1957	Dorothy L. Sayers (the Lord Peter Wimsey writer) died at her Witham home.
19 December 1982	A Townsend-Thoresen ferry capsized off Harwich.
20 December 1890	Joseph Leatherdale was murdered by his nephew Arthur, aged eighteen, at Salcott.
21 December 1762	Explorer Captain Cook married Essex girl Elizabeth Batts at St Margaret's, Barking.
22 December 1948	Noel Edmonds born in Ilford.
23 December 1927	Ebenezer Mather, founder of the Royal National Mission to Deep Sea Fishermen, died on Canvey Island.
24 December 1998	Last episode of *Birds of a Feather*, the television show that put Chigwell on the map.
25 December 855	Edmund was crowned King of the East Angles at Bures.
26 December 1985	The last dog race took place at Southend's greyhound stadium.
27 December 1919	John Groom died at Clacton-on-Sea in one of the orphanages he founded.
28 December 1934	Actress Maggie Smith born at Clayhall.
29 December 1860	Britain's first iron-hulled warship, HMS *Warrior*, was launched by Thames Ironworks.
30 December 1901	Brightlingsea station destroyed by fire.
31 December 1941	Actress Sarah Miles born at Ingatestone.

ACKNOWLEDGEMENTS

Apart from Michelle Tilling at The History Press, who gave me just the right amount of time to finish this project, I would like to thank all those research junkies in libraries all around Essex. My motto, as always when researching, is 'need something verified, ask a librarian.' Jonathan Hughes at Redbridge, Karen Jones at Chelmsford and Simon Donoghue at Romford deserve a special mention, although everyone at Answers Direct and at the Essex Record Office has also been helpful when facts needed corroborating. In addition, some local history writers such as Judith Williams, Linda Rhodes, Mavis Sipple, John Debenham and Patrick Denney, are always happy to assist. Supportive friends include Pat Stone, Donna Lowe, Kim Kimber and Deborah Campagna – and not forgetting my own personal proof reader, husband Raymond.

Any attempt at a bibliography would prove too hefty a task, as while the snippets in these pages may have originated in a book, a newspaper report, a document, or a website, they will have been followed up in other formats, so there may be three 'sources' for one paragraph. Needless to say, just about every book on Essex has been man- (or woman-) handled to some degree, including the many by such prolific writers as Stan Jarvis, and including the old (the eighteenth-century Philip Morant) and the new (Ian Yearsley). Also useful were many copies of the defunct *Essex Review* and *Essex Countryside* as well as the more contemporary *Essex Life* in libraries (where else?) and via that provider of all things: e-bay. *Local History Magazine* has proved an occasionally useful source, and the *Oxford Dictionary of National Biography* has been there when needed. Individuals who have helped to cross t's and dot i's include Hamish Walker, Jeremy Carter and David Nathan.

Illustrations were a little easier than they could have been, thanks to www.clipart.com and the help of Holly Thompson from Jupiter Images. The cartoons used, including those from *Punch*, are out of copyright, as far as it has been possible to establish. In the event of any oversight, please contact the author through the publisher. My drawings are on pp. 65 and 129, and Toby Williams was also able to supply a couple of illustrations to fill in the gaps (pp. 38 and 139). I have to thank Chris Strachan, Chairman of Trustees at Harwich Electric Palace Trust, for granting permission to use the cartoon by Marjorie Cornish featured in his book *The Harwich Electric Palace* (p. 9).

Dee Gordon, B.A. (Lit)

Note that information used is correct as far as could be ascertained at time of writing but some data liable to subsequent change.

Visit our website and discover thousands of other History Press books.

www.thehistorypress.co.uk